YOU'RE *Welcome* HERE

Embracing the
Heart of Hospitality

A six-week study based on the teaching of
NANCY DEMOSS WOLGEMUTH

© 2024 *Revive Our Hearts* Ministries

Published by *Revive Our Hearts* Ministries
P.O. Box 2000, Niles, MI 49120

ISBN: 978-1-959704-08-9

Printed in the United States of America.

All rights reserved. No part of this publication may be reproduced in any form without permission from the publisher, except in the case of brief quotations embodied in other works or reviews.

Adapted from the teaching of Nancy DeMoss Wolgemuth by Erin Davis and Katie Laitkep, edited by Mindy Kroesche and Mindi Stearns.

Cover design by Austin Collins. Typography and interior design by Lauren Davis.

Unless otherwise noted, all Scripture quotations are taken from the Christian Standard Bible®, Copyright © 2017 by Holman Bible Publishers. Used by permission. Christian Standard Bible® and CSB® are federally registered trademarks of Holman Bible Publishers.

Scripture quotations marked ESV are from The ESV® Bible (The Holy Bible, English Standard Version®), copyright © 2001 by Crossway, a publishing ministry of Good News Publishers. Used by permission. All rights reserved.

Scripture quotations marked (PME) are taken from the PHILLIPS MODERN ENGLISH BIBLE, by J. B. Phillips, "The New Testament in Modern English," Copyright© 1962 edition, published by HarperCollins.

All emphasis in Scripture has been added.

Contents

How to Use This Study	4
The Heart of Hospitality	5
Week 1: Your Home Is a Mission Field	6
Week 2: Evidence of Genuine Love	26
Week 3: God's Heart from the Start	46
Week 4: The Beauty of Hospitality	66
Week 5: Your Heavenly Home	88
Week 6: Your Most Honored Guest	108
Discussion Questions	128
Notes	130

HOW TO USE THIS STUDY

This is not just a book on the topic of hospitality. You won't find vintage recipes or napkin folding tricks tucked in its pages. The goal is to give you a guide to dig into God's Word and find *His heart for hospitality*. To get the most out of it, here are some basic tips for digging into Scripture.

The Bible is a book about God. As you study, don't jump to application too quickly. Take time to consider: What does this teach me about the heart of God?

Lead with prayer. Before you dive into each day's study, ask the Holy Spirit to give you wisdom and insight. Ask Him to help you understand biblical hospitality and give you opportunities to put what you're learning into practice.

Dig deeply. Since hospitality is, at its core, an invitation to connect, take your time. Read passages slowly and repeatedly. The more time and energy you invest in this study, the more you will get in return.

Learn together. Hospitality requires connection. Consider starting a small group in your home or gathering with other women once a week for coffee and to talk about what you've learned. Discussion questions for each lesson are included on page 128.

Study the key passage. Though you will study passages all throughout your Bible for this study, consider Romans 12:9–21 your anchor passage. Make an intentional effort to memorize these verses as you work through the content. Fill-in blanks throughout the study are based on the Christian Standard Bible®.

Press play. Supplementary video lessons for this study are available at ReviveOurHearts.com/hospitality. Join in as women in different seasons of life discuss the study and model biblical hospitality.

THE HEART OF HOSPITALITY
ROMANS 12:9-21

[9] Let love be without hypocrisy. Detest evil; cling to what is good. [10] Love one another deeply as brothers and sisters. Take the lead in honoring one another. [11] Do not lack diligence in zeal; be fervent in the Spirit; serve the Lord. [12] Rejoice in hope; be patient in affliction; be persistent in prayer. [13] Share with the saints in their needs; pursue hospitality. [14] Bless those who persecute you; bless and do not curse. [15] Rejoice with those who rejoice; weep with those who weep. [16] Live in harmony with one another. Do not be proud; instead, associate with the humble. Do not be wise in your own estimation. [17] Do not repay anyone evil for evil. Give careful thought to do what is honorable in everyone's eyes. [18] If possible, as far as it depends on you, live at peace with everyone. [19] Friends, do not avenge yourselves; instead, leave room for God's wrath, because it is written, Vengeance belongs to me; I will repay, says the Lord. [20] But

> If your enemy is hungry, feed him.
> If he is thirsty, give him something to drink.
> For in so doing
> you will be heaping fiery coals on his head.

[21] Do not be conquered by evil, but conquer evil with good.

Week 1
Your Home Is a Mission Field

Big Idea: You have been called to practice hospitality.

INTRODUCTION

Hers is the house you love to visit . . .

Her lawn is covered in manicured gardens, bespeckled with beautiful flowers. Her front door beckons you closer, adorned in a gorgeous wreath. The mat on the stoop announces "You are welcome here." She always answers the door with a smile.

"I'm glad you're here," she says. You can tell she means it.

The table looks like it's been set for a royal banquet. Warm cinnamon rolls and fresh coffee lure you in. *All of this for me?* you marvel. The tension in your neck relaxes. Now *this* is hospitality.

But what if you don't have a spacious home decorated to perfection? What if the last time you tried to cook, your kitchen filled with smoke instead of warm and inviting smells? Can you shrug your shoulders and tell yourself, "Hospitality just isn't my gift"?

The answer lies in your definition of hospitality. If glossy magazines or heart-worthy social media posts define the meaning of hospitality, most of us can never deliver. There are toys on the floor after all. Our furniture isn't new. Our laundry isn't folded. Our style doesn't match the current trends.

But what if we look to the Bible? What if we take God at His Word that true hospitality begins in the heart, then transforms how we use our homes? What if it's not reserved for the woman with the perfect house surrounded by the perfect lawn who makes perfect cinnamon rolls? What if hospitality is an assignment given to *all* of God's children? What if it's for *you*?

The Greek word for hospitality in the New Testament is *philoxenia*. Literally, it means to love the stranger.[1] As you begin this study, you'll see that hospitality is less of an obligation and more of an opportunity. Living with open hearts and homes puts the inviting nature of God on display. We *get* to welcome others because Christ has welcomed us. Your imperfect home can point others to a perfect God.

Spotlight
LYDIA

Lydia had a profound impact on the early church. Originally from Thyatira, Lydia was living in Philippi and was a dealer in purple cloth.

When Paul and his friends shared the gospel with Lydia, "the Lord opened her heart" (Acts 16:14) and she believed. She urged the men to stay at her house, giving them a base as they traveled throughout Philippi. Lydia's home became the meeting place for the first European church. She opened her door to bless others, and it became an important outpost for the gospel.

DAY 1: SET APART HOSPITALITY

Read Romans 12:9–21.

The book of Romans was written by the apostle Paul as he was wrapping up his third missionary journey. Having planted and established many churches in the east, the time had come for the westward expansion of the mission. His intent was to move his home base from Antioch to Rome, so he wrote a letter, paving the way for missional partnership with his Roman brothers and sisters in Christ.[2]

Much of Paul's ink was spilled on building a theological framework, but his purpose wasn't to fill the Roman's heads with mere knowledge. His letter reverberates with the question, "Now that we know what is true, how then shall we live?"

Paul's brass tacks answer is found in the first few pen strokes of his epistle.

Read Romans 1:1. How does Paul describe himself?

_____

_____

_____

What do you think it means to be "set apart for the gospel of God"? (If you get stuck look up 2 Timothy 2:21.)

_____

_____

As we turn from our sin and respond to God's invitation to forgive us, He transforms us into something new (2 Cor. 5:17). Every day provides a fresh opportunity to operate in ways that are distinctly different from those who do not know Christ. Nothing is out of reach of the Spirit's transforming power, including the way we operate within our homes.

After establishing himself as set apart because of the gospel, Paul went on to list the marks of a true Christian. Reread Romans 12:9–21. Using the chart below, make a list of the commands Paul gave placing them in the categories of Dos and Don'ts.

DOs	DON'Ts

These are not steps that must be taken to *earn* salvation but rather ways to intentionally showcase the work God has already graciously done in you.

Evaluate the list on the previous page. Put a star beside the action steps you are faithfully taking (example: holding fast to what is good). Place an arrow beside the steps where you see room for improvement.

Verse 13 describes two specific action steps. What are they?

___

Does this verse read more like a suggestion or a command? Explain your answer.

___

The word Paul originally used in the Greek language is a strong verb that means "to pursue, to strive for something." It suggests vigorous effort and intentionality.[3] As an outflow of being set apart in Christ, Scripture calls you to *pursue* hospitality. It's purposeful. Paul's exhortation is to think about it, pray about it, plan for it.

As you wrap up today's study, go back to the Dos and Don'ts chart. Pray through the list, asking God to help you live it out. Use the space below to record your prayer or any actions steps you feel led to take.

___

DAY 2: REAL DEAL LOVE

Read Romans 12:9–10.

Imagine it's late on Sunday morning. The pastor just dismissed you, and your family spills out into the lobby along with the other worshipers. These are your brothers and sisters in Christ. You love them. How do you show it? Do you smile and wave as you rush your family to the car? Do you linger a little longer than usual, asking routine questions like "How was your week?" or "What's new with you?"

What if you put love into action by opening your home? What if you spent the week praying about who you could invite over for a meal and willingly pushed past the awkwardness of forging a new friendship by welcoming someone new to sit at your family's table? Love requires action. That simple fact is the heartbeat of true, Christian hospitality.

Look at Romans 12:9 again. What kind of love does Paul urge followers of Jesus to express?

_____

_____

_____

Some translations say to love "without hypocrisy" (CSB), others say "let love be genuine" (ESV). The bottom line is the same. Hypocritical love gives lip service but requires nothing of you. Do you ever say you love your brothers and sisters in Christ but let inconvenience keep you from expressing your love in actions? Briefly explain your response.

_____

_____

_____

Why do you think Paul was compelled to write to the Christians in his day to avoid this kind of love?

_____
_____
_____

Write out 1 John 4:19 below.

_____
_____

Underline the number one reason we can and should show love to others. Though Jesus was not well received when He came to earth to save us, He put His love into action on the cross. This shifts our motivation for hospitality as we seek to love others.

Read John 15:12. How are we supposed to love others?

_____
_____

In what ways does Jesus demonstrate His love?

_____
_____
_____

An open heart and home is a practical way of loving others as an outflow of Jesus' love for you. This shift is important because it minimizes the aspects of hospitality that can cause the most stress: elaborate menu planning, spotless floors, quiet, well-behaved children, scintillating dinner conversation . . . None of those are required to show someone genuine love.

Can you think of a time when you experienced Christlike love because someone opened their home to you? Write about it below.

___

Ask the Lord to help you identify one person who needs to experience God's love today. What's one practical step you can take to show them hospitality?

___

DAY 3: THE ONE ANOTHERS

Read 1 John 3:23–24.

Start to look for them in your Bible, and you will find them everywhere—the "one anothers." They are a series of commands for how the children of God should treat each other.[4]

We find one here . . .

"Outdo one another in showing honor" (Rom. 12:10 ESV).

Another one here . . .

"Comfort one another" (2 Cor. 13:11 ESV).

And still another one right here . . .

"Confess your sins to one another and pray for one another" (James 5:16).

Pile all of the "one anothers" into one big, beautiful box, and you could wrap it neatly with this bow: "Now this is his command: that we believe in the name of his Son, Jesus Christ, and *love one another* as he commanded us" (1 John 3:23).

Love one another.

Perhaps it feels like an overly simplistic solution to a world so broken by sin. Or maybe, more likely, you've tried it and found the "others" in the "one anothers" difficult to love. And yet over and over throughout His Word, God repeats this command.

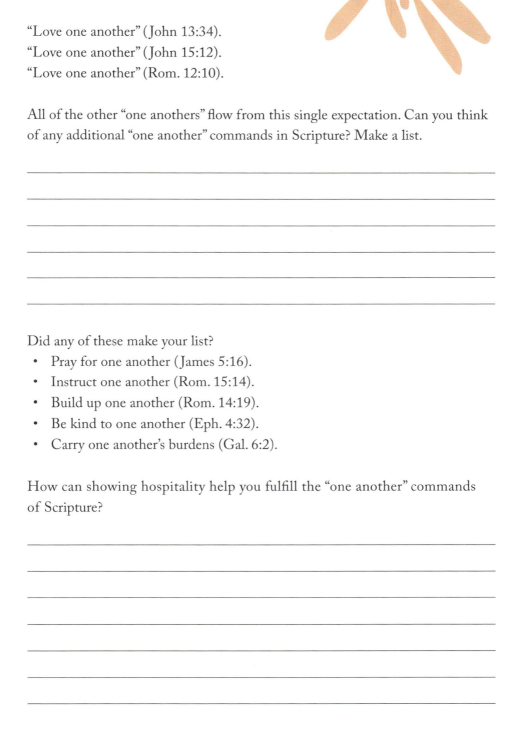

"Love one another" (John 13:34).
"Love one another" (John 15:12).
"Love one another" (Rom. 12:10).

All of the other "one anothers" flow from this single expectation. Can you think of any additional "one another" commands in Scripture? Make a list.

_____
_____
_____
_____
_____
_____

Did any of these make your list?
- Pray for one another (James 5:16).
- Instruct one another (Rom. 15:14).
- Build up one another (Rom. 14:19).
- Be kind to one another (Eph. 4:32).
- Carry one another's burdens (Gal. 6:2).

How can showing hospitality help you fulfill the "one another" commands of Scripture?

_____
_____
_____
_____
_____
_____

Compare and contrast 1 John 3:23–24 and Matthew 22:34–40 using the chart below. Underline any commands that are the same in both passages. Circle the word love wherever it appears in each passage. Draw arrows wherever the passages are communicating the same big idea.

1 John 3:23-24

23 Now this is his command: that we believe in the name of his Son, Jesus Christ, and love one another as he commanded us. 24 The one who keeps his commands remains in him, and he in him. And the way we know that he remains in us is from the Spirit he has given us.

Matthew 22:34-40

34 When the Pharisees heard that he had silenced the Sadducees, they came together. 35 And one of them, an expert in the law, asked a question to test him: 36 "Teacher, which command in the law is the greatest?"

37 He said to him, "Love the Lord your God with all your heart, with all your soul, and with all your mind. 38 This is the greatest and most important command. 39 The second is like it: Love your neighbor as yourself. 40 All the Law and the Prophets depend on these two commands."

Was Jesus saying we must show love to others as a way to earn salvation? Explain your answer.

_____

_____

_____

When Jesus was asked about the greatest commandment, what was His first answer (Matt. 22:37–38)?

_____

_____

Loving God is our first and most significant priority. As a result of His love for us, we are called to proactively love the people God puts into our lives.

Hospitality cannot save us from our sin: it is not a means to impress God. Instead we use the gifts God has given us—our time, our home, our resources—as a practical, ongoing way to showcase what God has done in our lives to the "one anothers" all around us.

Read Romans 13:8–10 (below) slowly and with the "one anothers" in mind.
- In verse 8, circle what the passage says we owe others.
- In verse 9, underline how we are commanded to carry this out.
- In verse 10, draw a line through what Christlike love is not/does not do.

> ⁸ Do not owe anyone anything, except to love one another, for the one who loves another has fulfilled the law. ⁹ The commandments, Do not commit adultery; do not murder; do not steal; do not covet; and any other commandment, are summed up by this commandment: Love your neighbor as yourself. ¹⁰ Love does no wrong to a neighbor. Love, therefore, is the fulfillment of the law.

When Paul wrote, "Love, therefore, is the fulfillment of the law" (v. 10), what did he mean? (Hint: look back at Matthew 22:34–40.)

_____

_____

_____

You could never invite enough people over to earn God's love. He already loves you! You could never serve a meal perfect enough to meet God's standard of perfection, but you can bless the "one anothers" in your life because God loves you. How does this reality affect your perspective on hospitality?

_____

_____

_____

_____

DAY 4: THE WHO OF HOSPITALITY

Read Isaiah 58:3–8.

Which of these are true about you today?

- [ ] You've laid aside your hangups about needing a perfect house to show biblical hospitality.
- [ ] You're ready to put love into action by opening your home.
- [ ] You agree with God's Word that hospitality makes a way for you to live out the "one anothers" of Scripture.

Scripture gives us the *why* of hospitality: it's a practical means to show God's love to others. It also gives us the *who*. As we look at several passages, make a list of the kinds of people the Bible specifically asks you to show hospitality to.

Show Hospitality To:

_____
_____
_____
_____
_____
_____
_____
_____
_____
_____
_____

Revisit Isaiah 58:3–8. In this passage, God expresses His anger toward the Israelites. How would you sum up His frustration toward His people?

_____

_____

Look again at verse 7. *With whom* did God want the Israelites to share their bread? Add them to the list at the start of today's study.

What are some things people hunger for other than food? How can hospitality satisfy that hunger?

_____

_____

_____

Read Job 31:32. *To whom* does this verse encourage you to open your door? Add them to the list.

Travelers need somewhere to stay. Showing hospitality means you won't miss the opportunity to share the love of Christ, to tear down walls, and to meet people at their point of need.

Read Romans 12:13 and identify *to whom* this passage tells us to show hospitality. What's another way to describe "the saints"? Add that to your list.

What needs do other Christians have? How can you meet those needs through hospitality?

_____

_____

Paul's letters are filled with encouragement to show Christian hospitality. Perhaps that was because he experienced the benefits of it so often. Look up the verses below and write down the names of individuals who showed hospitality to Paul.

Romans 16:1–2 _____

Romans 16:23 _____

Acts 16:25–34 _____

Acts 18:1–4 _____

As a missionary, Paul represents those serving in Christian ministry: pastors, missionaries, and volunteers. Just as Paul's ministry was supported by those who housed and cared for him, you can contribute to the work of Christian workers by welcoming them into your home.

Scripture also gives examples of Christians receiving nonbelievers in their homes as a way to share the gospel. Add unbelievers to the list above. Consider Matthew 9:9–12. Underline the kinds of people Matthew invited into his home. Highlight the message Matthew's guests heard from Jesus.

> ⁹ As Jesus went on from there, he saw a man named Matthew sitting at the tax office, and he said to him, "Follow me," and he got up and followed him.
>
> ¹⁰ While he was reclining at the table in the house, many tax collectors and sinners came to eat with Jesus and his disciples. ¹¹ When the Pharisees saw this, they asked his disciples, "Why does your teacher eat with tax collectors and sinners?"
>
> ¹² Now when he heard this, he said, "It is not those who are well who need a doctor, but those who are sick.

Look at the list you've compiled on page 18. Though it will require some effort, you may be eager to welcome weary travelers or Christian workers into your home. Yet true Christian hospitality stretches us outside of our comfort zones. Sometimes *way* outside of our comfort zones.

Read Romans 12:20–21. *Toward whom* does this passage tell you to reach? Add them to the list.

Biblical hospitality is not just for those who think like you. It's not just for those who will eagerly accept your invitation and shower you with gratitude after you've welcomed them into your home. It is a way to reach toward those who you struggle to get along with. Hospitality seeks to meet the needs of those who have hurt us because that's what Jesus did for us.

Christian history records that Polycarp, a Christian leader in Smyrna in the first century, showed this kind of radical hospitality to the Roman soldiers who arrested him. When the soldiers showed up at his door, Polycarp invited the soldiers in and fed them a meal. He prayed for them, then went without resistance as they led him to the trial where he received the death sentence.[5] In this way, he embodied Paul's command to "conquer evil with good" (v. 21).

Your enemies likely aren't the soldiers of an oppressive regime determined to silence your Christian witness. God's Word may hit closer to home when it comes to this principle. Perhaps it's someone at work who hasn't been kind to you or a friend who cut you out of her life without explanation. It could be a member of your family who has not made you feel welcome in their home. As you're reading these words, resistance is welling up in your heart: "Well, I don't feel welcome in their home. They've rejected me. They've rejected my child. They've rejected my husband. They're critical of me. . . ."

Jesus knows what it's like to experience that kind of hurt. Aren't you glad He still reached toward you and meets your needs? You can follow His example by showing hospitality to those who have hurt you. When you do, you are demonstrating Christlike love.

Reflect on the list you made on page 18. What kinds of people are you most likely to show hospitality to? Is there any group on your list that you've *never* invited into your home?

DAY 5: NO GONGING

Read Luke 10:38–42.

It's the frustration expressed under your breath . . .
It's the plates thrown onto the table a little harder than usual . . .
It's the deep sigh at the kitchen sink . . .

Sometimes the act of hospitality is not the problem; it's our attitude toward it.

Describe Martha's attitude toward hospitality in the passage you just read. Explain your answer.

_____
_____
_____

Have you ever had a "Martha moment," a time when your home was full but your heart was distracted? Write about it below.

_____
_____
_____

Consider 1 Peter 4:9. What qualifier does this verse give for true, Christian hospitality?

_____
_____

The Greek word for "grumbling" or "complaining" in this verse is *gongusmos*.[6] It's the word from which we get our word "gong." Scripture's clear call is to show hospitality without gonging, without making an unnecessary and irritating ruckus. Like Martha, it's possible to go through the motions of hospitality while grumbling about how much there is to do, how hard it is to cook and clean up after the meals, and what a mess your guests have made.

How does this violate the heart of hospitality the Bible calls us to?

_____

_____

_____

Write out the following verses:

2 Corinthians 9:6–7

1 Corinthians 10:31

1 Corinthians 16:14

How do these passages apply to the heart of hospitality?

_____

_____

_____

_____

Biblical hospitality is not a duty to perform as drudgery. It should be a delight. God loves a cheerful giver because He is happy to give generously to His children (Psalm 104:10–18; 2 Cor. 9:8–15). You can give your time, your resources, and your efforts with a genuine smile on your face knowing you are living out the call of Scripture. Instead of gonging—making a lot of unpleasant noise about the sacrifice you've made—your heart can express the beautiful music of gratitude and love.

To close out this week's study, write a prayer to God. Ask Him to reveal any attitudes you may have about hospitality that aren't pleasing to Him. Repent. Ask Him to increase your desire to love others well and to provide opportunities for you to open your home as a way to show His heart to those around you.

_____
_____
_____
_____
_____
_____
_____
_____
_____
_____
_____
_____
_____

Love does no wrong

to a neighbor.

Love,

therefore,

is the fulfillment

of the law.

—ROMANS 13:10

Week 2
Evidence of Genuine Love

Big Idea: Hospitality is a heart posture grounded in the gospel.

INTRODUCTION

You're having lunch with your family at a restaurant after a Sunday worship service when you hear the woman sitting behind you mention she had visited a church in the area. "It was my first time there," she says, "but I don't think I'm going back." You pry the bread basket out of your toddler's hands and lean back against the booth, trying to hear the woman's answer as her friend asks her what happened.

"The people just weren't friendly," the woman says. "I tried one of their Bible study classes, but no one said anything to me or even seemed to realize that I was there." She stops talking, and you think she's about to change the subject when you hear her quietly add, "It's embarrassing. When I got in my car, I just started crying. Honestly, I think I felt more lonely when I left than when I walked in."

You feel a pit in your stomach even before she stands up to leave—before you see her face and realize she had been visiting *your* class that morning.

Welcoming.
Warm.
Friendly.
Safe.

Aren't *those* the words you want people to use after they've spent time in your church? You want them to feel seen and loved—the last thing you want is for someone to leave feeling alone or rejected. You want her to walk away saying, "This is a church that feels like home."

Why? Because an unfriendly church is antithetical to the heart of the gospel. As followers of Christ, *we* are the Church. *We* are the family of God. *We* are brothers and sisters, called to reflect God's character to a watching world. When we fail to welcome others as Christ has welcomed us, we miss the opportunity to show those around us who He is. Embracing hospitality as a way of life helps make the gospel real to those around us.

Spotlight
PRISCILLA AND AQUILA

Priscilla and Aquila were working as tentmakers in Corinth when they first met Paul (Acts 18:1–2), who stayed with them and worked alongside them (v. 3). When God sent Paul to Ephesus, they went with him (v. 18). There they hosted a church in their home (1 Cor. 16:19) and were able to disciple a man named Apollos, who played a strategic role in spreading the gospel (Act 18:24–28). In Romans 16:5, they're mentioned as once again hosting a church in their home. The practice of hospitality was a way of life to them.

DAY 1: MOTIVATED BY MERCY

Read Romans 12:1–8.

Have you ever had a guest stay longer in your home than you originally planned? You invited them to stay for a night or two, never expecting that after a full week—or several weeks or even months later—you'd still be bumping into them in the middle of the night on your way to the bathroom.

You may feel comfortable if friends or family members ask to live with you while they're in town, recovering from a medical procedure, or undergoing temporary renovations. But what about when their stay doesn't come with a check-out date? How would it feel to invite people to move in—not just visit but come and live with you forever?

That's the heart of God. His mercy includes an invitation that says, *Come. I want you to live with me forever.* While we were still His enemies, He reconciled us through the death of His Son (Rom. 5:10) and adopted us into His family (Eph. 1:5).

Last week, we looked at the second half of Romans 12. Let's rewind to take a closer look at how this chapter begins.

Chapter 12 marks a major break in the book of Romans. Read Romans 12:1 in the CSB translation. What word does Paul use to begin this verse?

_____

_____

That first word is not a casual transition pivoting from a previous argument. It's a connector tying together *everything* that came before in Romans 1–11.

Therefore, Paul says, what are we to live in view of?

_____

How would you define mercy? Look up the word in the dictionary and write it below.

_____

_____

_____

Did you notice that the word "mercies" is plural in Romans 12:1? You'll find examples of the mercies of God in the following verses. Record what each one mentions that we have received from Him:

Romans 5:1 _____

Romans 5:10–11 _____

Romans 6:22 _____

Romans 8:15 _____

A paraphrase of Romans 12:1 says that we're to have "eyes wide open to the mercies of God" (PME). How have you seen God's mercies in your own life? Think through your story using the chart below:

WHAT MY LIFE WAS LIKE BEFORE CHRIST	WHAT CHRIST DID FOR ME	HOW MY LIFE HAS CHANGED BECAUSE OF CHRIST

Look back at Romans 12:1. What did Paul ask the believers to do in response to all God had already done?

_____
_____
_____

Fill in the blank with the word used to describe the kind of worship Paul mentioned:

"Therefore, brothers and sisters, in view of the mercies of God, I urge you to present your bodies as a living sacrifice, holy and pleasing to God; this is your _____ worship."

As you think back on the ways that God has shown you mercy, why would it be logical for you to present yourself—your body, your heart, and all that you have—to Him as an act of worship?

_____
_____
_____

The mercies of God are meant to motivate everything you do. That's the framework Paul built before launching into the commands at the end of Romans 12.

Review Romans 12:9–21 by praying it back to the Lord. Write out your prayer below, and ask Him to help you live each command as an act of worship.

_____
_____
_____
_____
_____

DAY 2: A WAY WORTHY

Read Romans 16.

Christianity was never intended to be a solo endeavor. The choice to follow Christ is a personal decision, but the early church understood that we were made to live as one body of believers. Through small groups of believers meeting in homes, God multiplied the message of the gospel and used those individuals to change the world.

Romans 16 shows us a group of individuals who used their unique gifts to serve one another. As you read the following verses, consider why Paul chose to include them. *Circle* the names of each individual and underline the reason they were mentioned.

> ¹ I commend to you our sister Phoebe, who is a servant of the church in Cenchreae. ² So you should welcome her in the Lord in a manner worthy of the saints and assist her in whatever matter she may require your help. For indeed she has been a benefactor of many—and of me also.
>
> ³ Give my greetings to Prisca and Aquila, my coworkers in Christ Jesus, ⁴ who risked their own necks for my life. Not only do I thank them, but so do all the Gentile churches. ⁵ Greet also the church that meets in their home. Greet my dear friend Epaenetus, who is the first convert to Christ from Asia. ⁶ Greet Mary, who has worked very hard for you.

In the profile at the beginning of this week, you read about Priscilla and Aquila. How did Paul refer to them in Romans 16:3?

_____

_____

In verse 5, what did he say happened in their home?

_____

Acts 2:46–47 provides a picture of what happened when the early church met together. Summarize it below.

_____

_____

_____

The believers enjoyed fellowship together in their everyday environments. Picture your own home: your living room, your kitchen, or even the passenger seat of your car. Have you ever used one of these settings for discipleship? Explain your answer.

_____

_____

_____

Priscilla and Aquila had the opportunity to disciple a man named Apollos. How does Acts 18:24–26 describe him?

_____

_____

_____

_____

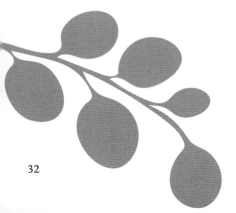

Acts 18:26 says that when Priscilla and Aquila heard Apollos, they took him aside and received him with open hearts. They knew he needed to be taught, but they did so sensitively. The impact was tremendous. Their example shows that the heart of hospitality extends beyond opening the door of your home. After Priscilla and Aquila "explained the way of God to him more accurately," what was the fruit of their investment in Apollos' life according to verses 27–28?

_____

_____

_____

_____

Priscilla and Aquila pulled Apollos *in* before sending him *out*. God used what happened in their home to impact countless others outside of it.

Think about someone you are currently mentoring or who you hope to begin mentoring. This may be a younger woman from church, a friend, or your own children. If someone were to write about your relationship the way that Paul summarized the story of Priscilla, Aquila, and Apollos in Acts 18, what would you hope would be said about your time together? Fill in the blanks below with your dream outcome.

After _____ (*your name*)

took _____ (*the name of the person you are mentoring*) aside and explained the way of God

to her, then _____

_____.

DAY 3: HOSPITALITY BEGINS AT HOME

Read Galatians 5:16–23.

If cameras were set up to secretly record what happens in the hours before you host an event, what would they capture? Whether you're preparing for a large holiday family gathering or just for a friend to stop by, does chaos seem to break out in the final countdown before people arrive?

With thirty minutes to go, you start throwing everything into a closet. You make passive aggressive (or aggressive-aggressive) comments to your roommate or husband about the dirty clothes they've left on the floor. You screech at your kids to come help as you run down the hallway, red-faced and frustrated.

Then the doorbell rings, and you open the door, smiling and warm and welcoming. To your guests, you're hospitable. But what would your family or roommates say?

On the left side of the chart below, add words that describe the way that people from church would describe you. On the right side, write a list of words from the perspective of those who live with you, whether it's your husband, children, or a roommate. (If you want to take it a step further, ask them!)

AT CHURCH	AT HOME

What do you notice about the two columns? If there are differences, why do you think that is?

_____
_____
_____
_____

Read Galatians 5:16–23. In verse 16, what command did Paul give?

_____
_____

The verb "walk" is literally translated "keep on walking."[1] As you move throughout your day, you have opportunities to depend on the indwelling Holy Spirit to help you serve your family in a way that honors God.

You won't be able to pursue hospitality at home without the Spirit working in you. But through His help, you'll experience good fruit—and your family will too.

Read John 13:12–15. Briefly describe what is happening in this scene.

_____
_____

What does Jesus say His followers ought to do?

_____
_____

Jesus set a high standard that He expects us to follow. He calls us to humbly serve one another.

Write out Matthew 23:12 below.

_____

_____

When we show hospitality to our guests, they may compliment and affirm our service in ways we don't always hear from our own families. But as followers of Christ, we are called to humble ourselves and serve regardless of the outcome. We may not receive in-the-moment gratitude from the people we serve, but Jesus promised that "whoever humbles himself *will be exalted.*"

What do you think Jesus meant by that promise?

_____

_____

Read Colossians 3:23–24. Ultimately, who are you serving through hospitality? What difference does it make to keep this perspective in mind?

_____

_____

_____

_____

Read Psalm 100:2. What should be the heart attitude of the one who serves?

_____

_____

_____

When you serve the Lord with a glad heart, your attitude has the power to transform the atmosphere in your household. Circle all of the words that describe the kind of environment you hope will be true of your home.

COZY   CHAOTIC   WELCOMING   COMFORTABLE

INVITING   STRESSFUL   WARM   DISORGANIZED

SERENE   DREARY   LOUD   COLD   CLUTTERED

PEACEFUL   ORGANIZED   VIBRANT

HARMONIOUS   DARK   JOYFUL

It's possible, with the help of the Spirit of God, to cultivate a home environment marked by the attributes you circled above.

Lord, help us to minister grace, encouragement, peace, and strength in our homes. Fill us with Your Spirit so that our homes may reflect the beauty of Your ways. I pray in Jesus' name, amen.

DAY 4: "AS SOON AS" BEGINS NOW

Read Matthew 14:1–18.

Two weeks into this study, you may find yourself thinking, "Lord, I want to be hospitable, but look at my schedule!" You're not the only one who feels this way. It's tempting to take notes with the intention of putting all of this into practice *as soon as* your life calms down.

Or if you're a single woman, *as soon as* you get married.
Or if you have kids, *as soon as* their sports season ends.
Or if you're taking care of elderly parents, *as soon as* your mother-in-law is back on her feet.

Go ahead and get all of your reasons for waiting, every "as soon as" you can think of, and write them down in the space below.

_____
_____
_____
_____

Jesus knew what it was like to face limitations during his life on earth. He was bound by the same twenty-four-hour cycle to accomplish His to-do list. He faced exhaustion and hunger and grief. In Matthew 14:13, Jesus received news about John, His cousin.

Reread Matthew 14:1–12. Briefly summarize what happened to John the Baptist.

_____
_____
_____

When you are facing grief or heartache, how does that impact your desire to be hospitable to others?

_____

_____

_____

When Jesus heard about John (Matt. 14:13), He and His disciples withdrew. They did not even have time to eat (Mark 6:31). But instead of finding a few minutes to be by themselves, the crowds found where Jesus was going and followed Him.

Read Matthew 14:14. What was Jesus' response to the people?

_____

_____

Jesus could have sent the people away at this moment, telling them to return as soon as the circumstances were better, but He had a mission to fulfill. As the day turned into evening, He had yet another opportunity to send the people away. In Matthew 14:15, what suggestion did the disciples give to Jesus?

_____

_____

_____

It's not that the disciples *weren't* concerned about the crowd's need to eat. They were simply being realistic: they were in a deserted place, likely several miles from the village.[2] When the disciples described the food situation, they did so in terms of their severely limited provisions. When Jesus responded, He spoke as though a large supply of food was available. And it was.

According to verse 20, what was the outcome of Jesus' miracle?

_____

_____

Jesus' hospitality in feeding the crowd was only a taste of what He would accomplish on an even greater scale. Isaiah 55:1–2 foreshadowed the salvation in Christ that satisfies believers' every spiritual need.

Read Isaiah 55:1–2. What word is repeated?

_____

Jesus offered a similar invitation in Matthew 11:28. In that verse, what did Jesus invite the weary and burdened to do?

_____

_____

You may not feel you have what you need to serve others in this season. It's true that your time, energy, and emotional capacity are limited—but you have access to a limitless God.

Read Philippians 4:13–14. What did Paul reveal about God? What did he say about how God uses people?

_____

_____

Revisit your "as soon as" list. How does knowing that God is able to provide in the midst of your limitations change how you approach hospitality?

_____

_____

_____

DAY 5: HOW BIG IS YOUR LOVE?

Read Luke 10:25–37.

Deep in the shadows of your attic, or back in a corner of your basement, do you have a stack of bins threatening to topple over? Each one contains decades of decorations: from autumn wreaths and a Christmas tree to cross displays for Easter.

These plastic storage containers can be a sign of just how much you love the holidays. Genuine love for *people* can't be measured in quite the same way. However, if you want to know how big your love is, look for concrete evidence of it in your hospitable actions toward your neighbor.

In Luke 10:25–37, who approached Jesus, and what did he ask?

_____

_____

Jesus responded to the religious expert by asking *him* a question: "What is written in the law?" (v. 26). What did the man say was written in the law?

_____

_____

In verse 25 and verse 29, we see the real reasons that this religious expert questioned Jesus. What reasons were given?

_____

_____

The religious expert thought he understood God's standard, but he was still trying to achieve it. "What must I *do*?" he asked. In response, Jesus told the parable of the good Samaritan. As you read these verses, notice that Jesus didn't provide a list of people to whom the expert should have gone out and served. Instead, the parable challenged the *kind* of neighbor the man was.

Describe the first two characters mentioned in the parable:

Verse 31: The Priest _____

Verse 32: The Levite _____

In contrast to the others, what did the Samaritan have in verse 33?

_____
_____

List the tangible ways the Samaritan demonstrated compassion.

_____
_____

Have you ever had someone physically care for you when you were sick or injured? Has anyone ever generously provided to help you meet financial needs? Describe the circumstances.

_____
_____
_____
_____

When you think about the parable, which character do you most identify with?

_____
_____
_____

Before Jesus began the parable, the religious expert addressed Jesus with the arrogance of one who believed he had held up God's standard to love his neighbor as himself.

Read Matthew 20:26–28 below.

> ²⁶"It must not be like that among you. On the contrary, whoever wants to become great among you must be your servant, ²⁷ and whoever wants to be first among you must be your slave; ²⁸ just as the Son of Man did not come to be served, but to serve, and to give his life as a ransom for many."

According to this passage, what did Jesus come to do? Underline it.
What did He not come to do? Circle it.

How do you see this truth illustrated in Jesus' parable about the Good Samaritan?

_____
_____
_____

Does this parable connect to what God's Word teaches about hospitality? Explain your answer.

_____
_____
_____
_____

We have all failed to be the kind of neighbor God has called us to be. The good news is that the gospel is not just a means of transportation to heaven; it's also a means of *transformation*, making us more like Jesus today. God is able to reshape our love so that we can reflect His heart in concrete ways to our neighbor.

If someone were to measure your love by how hospitable you are toward other people, how big would your love be today? Shade in the chart below.

Only Jesus fulfilled the perfect standard of love the law required. By His grace and with His example in front of us, may our love keep on growing more and more (Phil. 1:9).

Father, You have shown Your love by opening Your heart to us. Now You call us to show Your love in this world that is so broken and so wounded. Thank You for those who have opened their hearts to us and ministered Your grace. Please show us how to share Your love with others as we open our homes and extend hospitality for Jesus' sake, so they may know how much He loves them. In Jesus' name, amen.

Whatever you do,
do it from the heart,
as something done for the Lord
and not for people,
knowing that you
will receive the reward
of an inheritance
from the Lord.
You serve the Lord Christ.

—COLOSSIANS 3:23–24

Week 3
God's Heart from the Start

Big Idea: Focusing on God as our gracious Host helps us get over our hospitality hang-ups.

INTRODUCTION

Have you ever seen one of those shows where the head of a large corporation disguises his physical appearance and visits the lowest-paid employees? Sometimes it's the owner of thousands of restaurant chains who dons a mustache and steps up to the hostess stand at a rural location.

The local waiters, of course, have no idea who is standing in front of them as they welcome this man and his guests inside. But you do, as the viewer watching from home, so you cheer on the employees who are doing their job well and cringe when others display bad attitudes. From your spot on the couch, you want to shake every grumpy chef and say, "Don't you know who you're serving?!"

As followers of Christ, the stakes are even higher. Hebrews 13:2 says, "Don't neglect to show hospitality, for by doing this some have welcomed angels as guests without knowing it." In the ancient world, strangers were viewed as people who were "almost sacred, under God's special protection."[1] Throughout Scripture, we find commands and encouragement to welcome guests in the same way.

We see in the Old Testament that the people of God were expected to display a hospitable heart—*His* hospitable heart. This trait marked Israel in a way that set them apart from neighboring nations. With God as their model Host, it was unthinkable that they would refuse to welcome guests.

Spotlight
ABRAHAM

In Genesis 18:1–8, Abraham was sitting at the entrance of his tent, resting from the desert heat, when he saw three men. His immediate response was to offer them food, water, and a place to rest. He didn't think twice about extending hospitality because for him, it was a way of life.

Abraham was attentive to the practical needs of his guests. He and Sarah were willing to put in the effort to prepare a meal and share what they had. Abraham was a spontaneous and flexible host with an open tent and an open heart.

DAY 1: AN UNEXPECTED VISIT

Read Genesis 18:1–8.

When your neighbor shows up at your door with fresh cookies she's made . . .
When your mother-in-law arrives at your house an hour before your event starts . . .
When you get a text from a friend saying she's had a bad day and needs to come over . . .

How do you handle those unexpected visits?

Think back to the last time someone dropped by your house without notice. When they showed up at your door, how glad were you to see them? Place an X on the line below.

|———————————————————————————————|

UNHAPPY   **EXCITED**

In Genesis 18, Abraham received unexpected visitors. In verse 1, who does the author say appeared to Abraham?

_____

_____

When Abraham looked up and saw three men standing near him, what did he do?

_____

_____

_____

_____

Verses 6–7 reveal Abraham's eagerness in response to his guests. Underline all words that reference speed or urgency:

> ⁶ So Abraham hurried into the tent and said to Sarah, "Quick! Knead three measures of fine flour and make bread." ⁷ Abraham ran to the herd and got a tender, choice calf. He gave it to a young man, who hurried to prepare it.

When Abraham addressed his visitors with, "If I have found favor with you, please do not go on past your servant," he was saying, in effect, "You have done a great honor by visiting me. It's a privilege that you would come to my tent."

"Oh, what a blessing!" is often not our first reaction to surprise guests. When you think back to your last visitor, were you hesitant to receive them? Why or why not?

_____

_____

_____

_____

In Genesis 18, Abraham's focus was on the people who arrived and who he had the opportunity to serve. Though his ancient Middle East context had profound differences in their attitudes toward hospitality, his example still has much to teach us. In Abraham's nomadic lifestyle, visitors were either a threat or a delight, though rarely, if ever, a nuisance. Abraham was not concerned with himself or whether his home was ready for company but on making these individuals feel welcome. Through his response he communicated, "I am glad you're here. It is my joy to serve you."

Abraham's response foreshadowed the way Jesus responded to people who seemingly interrupted His schedule.

Next to each passage, write who interrupted Jesus in the middle column and how He responded in the right column. Imagine the outcome if Jesus had not received those who seemingly interrupted Him.

MARK 2:1–12		
MARK 5:24–34		
MARK 10:46–52		

Do you struggle to embrace unexpected guests? In the space below, list some of the people who are most likely to interrupt your routine. Next to each one, jot down a way that God might want to use that inconvenient moment to minister to the individual.

LIKELY TO INTERRUPT	WAY THAT GOD MIGHT WANT TO USE THE INCONVENIENT MOMENT

DAY 2: GIVING YOUR BEST

When you think of the life of Abraham, what comes to mind?

_____

_____

- Maybe you thought of his faith in following God from his homeland (Gen. 12:1–4).
- Or his belief in trusting the promises that God made to him (Gen. 17:1–27).
- Or his unwavering obedience in sacrificing Isaac (Gen. 22:1–18).

The Jews of Jesus' day thought of Abraham, their father in the faith, as the supreme model of hospitality. While Genesis 18 is not a passage specifically intended to instruct us about hospitality, it has much to say about how we welcome others.

Read Genesis 18:4–5. From the moment his guests arrived, Abraham was completely at their service. What were the first things he offered them?

_____

_____

These visitors had been traveling and were likely worn out, hungry, and thirsty. Abraham was attentive and tuned in to how he could meet their practical needs. In this ancient culture, it was common for a good host to provide both water for refreshment and the washing of dirty feet.

Read Genesis 18:6–8 and create a to-do list based on the meal preparations described in these verses.

-
-
-
-

There's effort involved in extending hospitality, and Abraham didn't cut corners. The extravagant banquet he prepared required work.

Consider what it communicates to your guests when you have dedicated the time to provide for them in an intentional way. Can you think of a time when someone cooked you a special meal? What was the context, and why was it meaningful?

_____
_____
_____

Note that Abraham did not act alone. Who else helped him prepare the feast for the guests?

_____
_____

Who is normally involved when you prepare a meal for guests?

_____
_____
_____

If you have children, it can often create more work to include them. If you are single and live with a roommate, it may be inconvenient to arrange for that roommate to help you. But beyond having extra hands available, why do you think it is worthwhile to include others in the process?

_____
_____
_____
_____

Read Genesis 18:8. Fill in the blank:

"He _____ them as they ate under the tree."

Your Bible may include a note next to the word "served" in verse 8. This verse may also be translated to say, "Abraham was *standing by them* as they ate." Abraham was not only a host, he was a waiter, selflessly tending to their needs.

Do you think Abraham deserves the title of model host? Explain.

_____
_____
_____

Despite cultural differences, what can you learn from the life of Abraham about receiving unexpected visitors?

_____
_____
_____
_____

In our modern, fast-paced culture you can follow Abraham's example by responding graciously to other kinds of interruptions. How can you show hospitality the next time your child needs your attention when you are focused on a task? How can you demonstrate God's love when a coworker drops by your desk? Or when someone texts to unload a burden they're carrying? As you head into your day, ask God to help you respond to others in love, even when they interrupt your plans.

DAY 3: THE ONES WHO WEAR HIS LOVE

Read Deuteronomy 10:12–22.

As a kid, did your parents sometimes remind you that when you stepped out the front door, you were representing the family? You wore *their* last name—and you were expected to wear it well.

The Israelites were given a similar mantle to carry. As those who represented God's name, they were to be hospitable because that's who He is. Once you start looking for this attribute of God in the Old Testament, you'll find it everywhere.

Read Deuteronomy 10. In this chapter, Moses called the people of Israel to love the Lord and commit themselves fully to His ways. Write down the words and phrases Moses used to describe God in verse 17.

_____

_____

_____

How can hospitality be a means to represent this awe-inspiring God well?

_____

_____

_____

Fill in the blank with the verb that summarizes what God's people are to do to imitate Him:

"You are also to _____ the resident alien, since you were resident aliens in the land of Egypt" (Deut. 10:19 CSB).

Moses was reminding the people, "God took care of you and brought you into His home. He was a host to you when you needed to be cared for. Therefore, you are to do likewise for others who need it." This is the same idea that Jesus shared when an expert in the law quizzed Him about what is the greatest commandment.

Read Matthew 22:34–40, then write out verse 39 below:

_____
_____
_____

What does it mean to love your neighbor as yourself? Dr. John Piper said it this way:

> As you long for food when you are hungry, so long to feed your neighbor when he is hungry. As you long for nice clothes for yourself, so long for nice clothes for your neighbor. As you work for a comfortable place to live, so desire a comfortable place to live for your neighbor. As you seek to be safe and secure from calamity and violence, so seek comfort and security for your neighbor. As you seek friends for yourself, so be a friend to your neighbor. . . . As you would that men would do to you, do so to them.[2]

When your son's best friend runs into your house after playing in the backyard, do you welcome him in and offer him a snack? When a coworker needs comfort and advice, are you generous in giving her your time and attention? Do you sometimes make extra food for dinner to share with the single mom next door, knowing it would bless her not to have to worry about a meal that night? You likely have more opportunities to show sacrificial, generous love than you realize.

The Old Testament people of God reflected His character to the world by imitating the love and hospitality He first showed them. As Christians—"little Christs"—we're to do the same. "We love because he first loved us" (1 John 4:19).

DAY 4: HOSPITALITY HANG-UPS

Read Psalm 78.

God is gracious and generous toward His people. It is unthinkable that He could be considered anything other than that. But we still doubt His ability to provide for our needs. It is unimaginable that God's people would be anything other than hospitable in light of all He has done. And yet we often are. Just like the Israelites who wandered in the desert, we can have an attitude of scarcity that leads to stinginess and prevents us from investing our time and energy in others. Let's think honestly about what's keeping us from extending hospitality.

Review Psalm 78:19–20 and describe Israel's doubts.

_____
_____
_____

In verse 21, what did God do in response to Israel's complaints?

_____
_____
_____

Psalm 78:22 shares why the Lord responded the way He did. What does it say?

_____
_____
_____
_____

Review Psalm 78:21–25. Even though the people doubted His ability to provide, what kind of provision did God ultimately give them?

_____
_____
_____

Aren't we just like the Israelites? We doubt the Lord's ability to meet our needs, and this doubt can show up in the way we approach our own acts of hospitality.

Do fear, comparison, materialism, or cost keep you from serving others? Next to each category that follows, circle the number to show how much of a struggle this area is for you. A rating of 0 signifies that it is not a concern, while a rating of 5 indicates a significant challenge or difficulty.

FEAR   0   1   2   3   4   5

Sometimes we're fearful that our actions will look stupid, we'll be embarrassed, that a meal or an event won't turn out as we hoped, or that we'll take a step toward loving someone and be rejected.

When it comes to hospitality, what are you afraid of?

_____
_____
_____

When we're afraid, we see the thing that we're afraid of as big and our capacity as small. We may believe that our embarrassment will be too much for us to handle, so we avoid anything that might cause it.

But we are to fight big fears with something even bigger: God's strength and sovereignty.

Read Psalm 63:3–5, then write a prayer asking the Lord to make you confident in knowing that He is in control and He can be trusted.

_____
_____
_____
_____
_____
_____

> If there is anything holding you back, or any sacrifice you are afraid of making, come to God and prove how gracious your God is.[3]
> —Andrew Murray

There will always be someone who has a nicer home, calmer kids, or less of a mess to deal with. But your home—the one God has given *you*—is intended to be a place used to extend grace to others.

COMPARISON   0   1   2   3   4   5

What areas of your home and family life are you most likely to compare to others? How does this hinder your willingness to show hospitality?

_____
_____
_____
_____

You may have little to offer your guests, but if you give them peace and joy and the presence of Christ then it doesn't matter whether you're serving caviar or canned soda. What you extend can be a meaningful gift to your guests if the Spirit of God is evident.

MATERIALISM   0 1 2 3 4 5

This can swing two different ways. We can be protective over what we have—so much so that we value our items more than people. We start to worry something will get ruined or stolen when we have guests over. These concerns reveal a heart consumed with temporal things. But we can also be ashamed of the little that we have or feel that we do not have what we need to be able to serve others.

Which side of this spectrum are you more likely to fall on?

_____
_____

What advice is given in 1 Timothy 6:17–19?

_____
_____
_____

Hospitality doesn't have to be expensive, but it will cost you. It will cost you money, time, energy, and comfort, but you have God's promise that He will reward you (Prov. 19:17).

COST   0 1 2 3 4 5

What has hospitality cost you in the past?

_____
_____
_____

Consider the blessings you could be missing out on if hospitality is not a way of life. God desires to reveal Himself and His heart through you.

Your hospitality hang-ups likely won't disappear overnight, but the God who is faithful to you today will be faithful to you when they emerge again. You alone know what your weaknesses are, so address them here, filling the space with reminders of truth that will strengthen your heart to make hospitality a way of life.

_____
_____
_____
_____
_____
_____
_____
_____

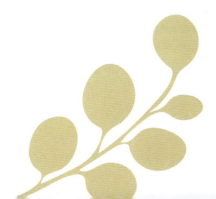

DAY 5: THE ULTIMATE HOST

Read Psalm 23.

Psalm 23, considered to be "perhaps the most famous poem in the history of the world,"[4] paints a picture of God as a gracious Host. Read the full psalm aloud with a highlighter in hand. Stop to note any details that reveal His hospitable heart to you.

> ¹ The Lord is my shepherd;
> I have what I need.
> ² He lets me lie down in green pastures;
> he leads me beside quiet waters.
> ³ He renews my life;
> he leads me along the right paths
> for his name's sake.
> ⁴ Even when I go through the darkest valley,
> I fear no danger,
> for you are with me;
> your rod and your staff—they comfort me.
>
> ⁵ You prepare a table before me
> in the presence of my enemies;
> you anoint my head with oil;
> my cup overflows.
> ⁶ Only goodness and faithful love will pursue me
> all the days of my life,
> and I will dwell in the house of the Lord
> as long as I live.

Using the details you highlighted, make a list of actions that God performs as our Host:

_____

_____

_____

_____

_____

In the first four verses of Psalm 23, David described being in green pastures beside quiet waters. Midway through the psalm, the scene changed. Describe the new setting we see in verse 5.

_____

_____

_____

_____

_____

This new scene is more intimate than the last, as the Lord allows David, the psalmist, to be His guest. In the face of David's impending danger, the Lord prepared a table before him. In other words, the Lord provided for him.

In Psalm 23:5, what does David say is done to his head?

_____

_____

This would have been a soothing act, and it is part of the picture of a host welcoming someone into his home.[5] In the Old Testament, it is a reference to blessing and honor. It meant that David was an honored guest.

In verse 5, what word describes the cup? What does this say about God's lavish love?

___

God isn't a stingy Host. He gives hospitality in abundance, overflowing with generosity.

How have you seen the Lord's generosity in your life?

___

Go back to Psalm 23. In verse 6, underline what it says about goodness and faithful love.

"Pursue me" implies seeking. It's not that those virtues chase us down on their own, but a good and merciful God pursues us and welcomes us. *This is hospitality.* When have you experienced God's pursuit?

Add three life events to the timeline below that highlight His goodness and mercy.

At the end of verse 6, where does David say he will dwell?

_____

What comes to your mind when you think of dwelling in the house of the Lord (v. 6)?

_____

_____

How long does David say that he will dwell in the house of the Lord?

_____

By itself, "as long as I live" is not an expression for eternity. But God is unable to break His covenant, which means that His commitment to His people will last forever. As Romans 8:38–39 says, "Neither death nor life, nor angels nor rulers, nor things present nor things to come, nor powers, nor height nor depth, nor any other created thing will be able to separate us from the love of God that is in Christ Jesus our Lord."

God is not only a gracious Host, He is the Ultimate Host . . . and His goodness and faithful love is ours forever. In the space below, write a psalm of gratitude praising Him for who He is. Then read it out loud to Him.

_____

_____

_____

_____

_____

_____

_____

*I will dwell
in the house of the LORD
as long as I live.*

—PSALM 23:6

Week 4
The Beauty of Hospitality

Big Idea: Our homes can be a picture of paradise.

INTRODUCTION

Do you ever find yourself getting caught up in the dramatic stories of Scripture?

You read the story of Abraham and think, *Yes, Lord! I'd follow you wherever You call me.* You follow the life of Daniel and pray, "Yes, Lord! I'd be willing to stand up for You no matter the cost!" You read the accounts of the disciples and the apostles in the Gospels and Acts and cry out, "Yes, Lord! I'll give You *all* that I have for the sake of Your name."

But then you're given an opportunity to live out those words, and you feel a twinge of panic. You suddenly regret not adding an asterisk to your previous prayers:

- Lord, I'm willing to use all that I have*
    *as long as my friends' toddlers don't spill anything on my new couch.
- Lord, I'm willing to host anyone in my home*
    *as long as they leave early enough for me to go to bed at a decent hour.
- Lord, I'm willing to invite my neighbor over for dinner*
    *as long as it's not the one night I have for self-care.

Hospitality will stretch you. It may cause you to wonder if what you're giving up is ultimately worth it, but surrender to the Lord is never in vain. God uses the sacrifices made through hospitality to increase your joy, make you more like Christ, and give those around you a glimpse of the eternal glories to come.

It's up to you. Will you choose to lay aside all asterisks as you live out biblical hospitality one "Yes, Lord!" at a time?

Spotlight
THE WIDOW OF ZAREPHATH

In 1 Kings 17, Israel was experiencing a severe drought and famine. God directed the prophet Elijah to visit a widow in Zarephath to ask for food. This woman had just enough left for one last meal for herself and her son. Despite her dire circumstances, she extended hospitality to Elijah, inviting him into her home, feeding him, and ministering to his needs before her own. As a result, God did a miracle and extended her food. For the entire time the famine lasted, her flour and oil never ran out (v. 16).

DAY 1: THE GOSPEL THROUGH GENEROSITY

Read Acts 4:32–37.

One cup of water. One couch. One empty room. What if God used your most ordinary possessions to advance the gospel throughout the world?

In the book of Acts, we read story after story of God's incredible grace and deliverance in the lives of the members of the early church. One of the most life-changing moments happened when a local community laid down their possessions.

In Acts 4:29–30, Peter and John were arrested and then released from custody. As the believers within their community faced persecution, they came together and prayed:

> [29] "Now, Lord, consider their threats, and grant that your servants may speak your word with all boldness, [30] while you stretch out your hand for healing, and signs and wonders are performed through the name of your holy servant Jesus."

Read Acts 4:31, and record what happened next.

_____

_____

_____

How is the group described in verse 32?

_____

_____

_____

Scholars note that the expression "of one heart and mind" pointed to real friendship: "As they prayed with one voice in verse 24, so now they are committed to each other in terms of resources."[1] Spiritual unity has a tangible impact.

Read Acts 4:34–35. What did the believers do with their resources?

_____

_____

Reread verse 34. What was the result of the believers' actions?

_____

_____

Can you imagine that? There was not a single needy person in the group.

Read Deuteronomy 15:4, and briefly summarize what it says.

_____

_____

_____

Generosity had been a standard of living that God had arranged beginning in the Old Testament, but it became a movement for the New Testament group of believers. The verb tenses "suggest a gradual liquidation of assets, not selling everything all at once."[2]

Within this community, many were poor, and others were facing isolation from their former communities due to persecution. How do you think this generosity impacted the faith of the new believers?

_____

_____

_____

Think about the last time another believer helped meet a need—big or small—in your life. Share the need, the person who provided help, and the impact it had on your faith.

_____
_____
_____

Read Acts 4:36–37. What did Joseph (a.k.a. Barnabas) do?

_____
_____

What is your initial reaction to his radical response?

_____
_____
_____

According to verse 37, where did he place the money?

_____
_____

The phrase "the apostles' feet" is used elsewhere in Scripture to express obedience or surrender of control.[3] How do you think that the idea of surrendering control connects to the idea of giving up your possessions?

_____
_____
_____
_____
_____

When has a need for control held you back from being generous toward others?

What are some additional reasons that you hold on to your possessions rather than using them for the purpose of service?

Acts 4:33 says, "With great power the apostles were giving testimony to the resurrection of the Lord Jesus, and great grace was on all of them."

The gospel is what made their generosity possible. These believers knew they had been given much through Jesus (Luke 12:48). The same God who raised Jesus from the dead met their spiritual needs. As they made their own costly sacrifices for the sake of meeting others' needs, their lives became a reflection of the gospel.

DAY 2: SHIPWRECKED!

Read Acts 28:1–10.

Do you know a woman who seems to be able to anticipate the needs of everyone around her? She always has extra snacks to give your kids. She has a fresh Kleenex for when you start to tear up and the right words of advice just when you're not sure what next steps to take.

Maybe you've watched her and wondered how she does it. You feel intimidated by what others are facing. You're not sure that if you reached toward others the way that she does, you'd really be able to make much of a difference.

But *you* wouldn't actually be the one to help her. As followers of Jesus, every need that you seek to meet is met through the Holy Spirit, at the will of the Father. Isn't that good news?

In the book of Acts, a group of people had the unexpected opportunity to meet the needs of a few misplaced travelers. Acts 27 ends with a dramatic scene on the sea that ended with the apostle Paul shipwrecked on a small island.

Read Acts 28:1–2. What actions did the local people take toward the travelers?

_____

_____

In verse 2, how is their hospitality described?

_____

_____

_____

The term for "kindness" used here only appears one other time in the New Testament.[4] Look up Titus 3:4–5 and write it below:

_____
_____
_____
_____
_____

How does the response of the people of Malta reflect the kindness of God?

_____
_____
_____

Read Acts 28:3–5. The scene is told from the perspective of the Maltese people. Do you think they had any regrets about extending hospitality to Paul?

_____
_____

Put yourself in their shoes. How do you think you would have handled the situation?

_____
_____
_____

The chief of the island also showed hospitality to the travelers. Describe what happened in Acts 28:7–10.

_____
_____

According to verse 10, when it was time to sail again, what happened?

The term for the Maltese people literally translates to "the barbarians." This same phrase was used to refer to non-Greek-speaking people.[5] The islanders were not uncultured, but they did not share the same background as Paul. In unusual circumstances, they showed extraordinary hospitality, and God worked through them to meet the travelers' needs. How much more could He use one of His own who is submitted to Him?

What does Matthew 6:32–34 reveal about God as a provider?

How could trusting God to be your provider impact your willingness to sacrificially serve others?

You likely won't be receiving shipwrecked houseguests with snakes hanging from their hands, but you may find yourself facing messy situations in your pursuit of hospitality. God may use the uncomfortable moments to teach you dependence on Him and to make you more like Jesus.

Maybe the people around you need someone to come alongside them in the midst of a season where they have seemingly shipwrecked their own lives through their choices. Maybe they need someone to disciple them more intentionally, or maybe they just need to know they have a safe place to stay if they ever need it.

You may not know exactly how you will respond when the situation arises, but you can trust that your God will supply all of *your* needs as you obey Him (Phil. 4:19). Take a few minutes to write a prayer thanking Him for this reality.

_____

_____

_____

_____

_____

_____

_____

_____

DAY 3: THE OTHER SIDE OF THE TABLE

Read Romans 12:9–21.

When it comes to serving, do you ever find that it's more difficult to receive hospitality than it is to provide it yourself?

_____

Imagine:

- A timer goes off in the kitchen, and you hear your daughter-in-law's footsteps as she runs into the living room with an update on dinner. You've been waiting for over an hour, and you know she still hasn't finished preparing the food. You offer to step in, but she insists you enjoy catching up with your son. You can't help thinking that it would be so much easier if you just took over and did it yourself.

- A woman at your church stops you in between services on a holiday weekend and hands you a small present she has made. The gift is sweetly given, but you didn't bring anything for her. It doesn't matter that she is expecting nothing in return—you spend the rest of the afternoon feeling guilty for not giving her anything and wondering how you'll return the favor.

- Your women's Bible study knows that you have a surgery coming up in just a few weeks. They graciously offer to provide you with meals while you are recovering. You thank them but say you'll be fine on your own.

What do you struggle with most when others step in to serve you?

_____
_____
_____

When Paul provided the commands in Romans 12, he issued them to a group of believers. They were meant to be lived out within a community. The same is true today: you're not the only one who has been called to walk out these principles.

Reread Romans 12:10 in the CSB translation. What does Paul say to take the lead in doing?

_____

He could have said: "Take the lead," and ended the command there. Instead, he gives a different approach, one similar to Philippians 2:3. Write that verse in the space below:

_____

_____

When it's time for you to be on the receiving end of hospitality, what do you think it means to consider others as more important than yourself?

_____

_____

This theme appears again in Romans 12:16. Fill in the blanks below based on the CSB version:

"Live in _____ with one another.
Do not be _____;
instead, associate with the _____.
Do not be _____ in your own _____."

Why is humility required to *receive* generous hospitality?

_____

_____

What are the areas of hospitality where you may be tempted to think more highly of your own skills than of those around you?

_____

_____

_____

Pride has a tendency to sneak in when we don't expect it—both when we are seeking to be hospitable and when we are on the receiving end of hospitality. Place a checkmark if any of the following have been true for you:

_____ Proud people focus on the failures of others and can readily point out those faults.
_____ Proud people are especially prone to criticize, and they talk to others about the faults they see.
_____ Proud people have to prove that they are right—they have to get the last word.
_____ Proud people are self-protective of their time, their rights, and their reputation.
_____ Proud people desire to be known as a success.
_____ Proud people have a feeling—conscious or subconscious—that "these people are privileged to have me and my gifts."
_____ Proud people have a drive to be recognized and appreciated for their efforts.
_____ Proud people get wounded when they are overlooked.
_____ Proud people are elated by praise and deflated by criticism.
_____ Proud people feel confident in how much they know and can do.
_____ Proud people are self-conscious; they worry about what others think of them.
_____ Proud people are concerned about appearing respectable.
_____ Proud people can't bear to fail or for anyone to think they are less than perfect.
_____ Proud people keep others at arm's length.[6]

Write a prayer below confessing the areas where you have been prideful when it comes to hospitality and ask the Lord to help you turn away from these actions. Use the checklist you just completed to get started.

_____
_____
_____

The only one who received the kindness of others perfectly was Jesus. Look up the following verses and note the situations where He received hospitality or service:

- John 12:1–7 _____
- Matthew 26:17–19 _____
- Mark 15:20–21 _____

A woman following Jesus' example is gracious and humble, whether she's at the head of the hostess table serving others or she has the opportunity to *receive* hospitality. Seeking to outdo each other in showing honor doesn't turn hospitality into a competition. One way you can love your brothers and sisters in Christ is to respond well when they seek to serve you.

Think of three situations you may encounter where you will have the opportunity to show honor as others serve you. Give a short description of how you hope to respond to each scenario:

-

-

-

DAY 4: THE BLESSINGS OF BEAUTY

Read Exodus 25:1–9.

As you have seen the Lord work in your heart throughout this study by revealing the spiritual importance of serving others within your home, you may have found yourself focusing more on the *invisible* aspects of hospitality.

That doesn't mean when you put down your Bible, pick up your phone, and scroll through picture-perfect images shared by influencers on social media that you aren't drawn to the beautiful decor. It doesn't mean that you haven't been distracted by the seasonal section of the last store you were in.

What are we supposed to do with the *physical* elements of hospitality? As followers of Jesus, are we only supposed to focus on meeting *spiritual* needs?

Before we look at how the Old Testament addressed this question, consider which side of the spectrum you're more likely to fall on. Do you get more caught up in decorating and cleaning to prepare your home for guests? Or do you tend to neglect the physical aspects of preparation and focus on the spiritual?

Place an X on the line to show where you tend to focus more time and energy.

|—————————————————————————————————|

PHYSICAL   **SPIRITUAL**

In the book of Exodus, God gave His people important instructions for a construction project that would change their nation.

Read Exodus 25:8. What were the people to make and what was the purpose of it?

_____
_____
_____

The tabernacle ("sanctuary" in CSB) was the symbolic dwelling place for God. Read Exodus 29:42–43. What took place in the tabernacle?

_____
_____
_____

In Exodus 25, the Lord described what materials were needed to build His earthly dwelling place. As you read verses 3–7, put on your project-manager hat. How would you categorize the various materials? Use the space below to sort them into groups of your choosing.

Go back to the items you listed.
- Use a highlighter to mark each *color*.
- Underline the various *textures*.
- Circle words related to *smell*.

The tabernacle's instructions were filled with beauty and order because this was the place where people would meet with God. *The physical space was a visual representation of His nature.*

Review Psalm 27:4 (CSB) and fill in the missing line:

> I have asked one thing from the LORD;
> it is what I desire:
> to dwell in the house of the LORD
> all the days of my life,
>
> _____
>
> and seeking him in his temple.

Consider what it would mean to you for someone to say, "I just love to come to your home because I feel like God is here." You reflect aspects of His presence when you welcome others with a hospitable heart. Even more, you can provide guests with a glimpse of the God you serve through your intentionality with the space He has given you.

Imagine you are a guest walking through your front door for the first time. What would you see?

_____
_____
_____
_____
_____

What does this first impression say to a guest? Does the atmosphere communicate chaos and disorder, or does it communicate peace, simplicity, beauty, and joy?

_____
_____
_____

Look back at Exodus 25:2. What quality was needed for those who gave materials for the tabernacle?

_____
_____

Your home will not always be perfectly presentable for guests. It won't be filled with the most expensive decorations or the most up-to-date designs, but even the simplest space can be a picture of the character of God if you are willing to allow Him to use it.

Are you willing?

DAY 5: A PICTURE OF PARADISE

Read Genesis 2:1–15.

Imagine you've been given a ticket to paradise. What image comes to mind when you envision your destination? A beach house beside sandy white shores? A mountain villa nestled between snow-capped peaks? A porch beside a peaceful lake? Those are the kinds of destinations that are often described as "heaven on earth."

What first comes to your mind when you think of paradise?

_____

_____

If you look the word "paradise" up in Merriam Webster's online dictionary, the first definition says that *paradise* has the sense of "Eden."

The account in Genesis 2 takes place before sin entered the world. This is the garden before suffering and brokenness. Using the details in that chapter as well as your imagination, step into the garden. Fill in the chart below with what you might have encountered using each of your five senses:

SIGHT	SMELL	TASTE	TOUCH	HEAR

Read Isaiah 51:3. What are some of the Edenic characteristics described in this verse?

_____
_____
_____

Did you observe that there are both spiritual and physical characteristics mentioned? The garden of Eden, much like our eternal home in heaven, had the joys and comforts that come with an uninhibited relationship with God, but it also had an explosion of color and beauty and song. God created *all* of our senses, and He intends for them to be enjoyed in a way that draws people closer to Him.

Think of a friend or family member's home that fills you with comfort whenever you have the chance to visit. What are some of the sensory details you've noticed in that space? Is there a cozy blanket you always grab? Soft lighting in the room? Gentle instrumental music in the background? A fragrant candle nearby? Fresh cookies waiting for you? Describe the atmosphere below.

_____
_____
_____
_____
_____
_____
_____
_____

As you've previously shown hospitality to others, you've likely incorporated some of these details. In the left hand column of the chart below, reflect on some of the ways you've ministered using the five senses in your own home. On the right side, brainstorm some ways that you could be intentional about using them in the future.

	HOW I'VE MINISTERED THROUGH THE FIVE SENSES	NEW WAYS TO SERVE MY GUESTS
SIGHT		
SMELL		
TASTE		
TOUCH		
HEAR		

When people enter your home, they are stepping away from their own world and all of its problems for a little while. You may look at your small apartment or house filled with loud kids and think, "This sure doesn't feel like heaven to me."

We live a long way from Eden, but as followers of Christ, heaven is coming.

Lord, take our small offerings—a warm cup of peppermint tea, art prints with Scripture on the walls, wind chimes on the porch—and use each one so that every guest will feel like she's encountering a piece of our eternal paradise (Luke 23:43).

> "Seek first the kingdom of God and his righteousness, and all these things will be provided for you."
>
> —MATTHEW 6:33

Week 5
Your Heavenly Home

Big Idea: Jesus is preparing a place for you.

INTRODUCTION

There's a difference between "I saved you a seat" and "I've been preparing for this day for weeks." While both express a welcome sentiment, the latter implies intentionality. It's your host going to the trouble to make your favorite meal.... It's a piece of chocolate with the note she leaves on your pillow.... It's stocking the guest bathroom with toiletries you may have forgotten....

Biblical hospitality goes the extra mile to serve others for one simple and spectacular reason: Jesus went the extra mile to serve us.

As you read these words, He is busy preparing a place for you. Once the table has been set with a feast and the house is ready for arrival, He will come for you and welcome you into heaven, *His home*. Let this radiant hope shift how you see your own home and give you fresh inspiration to love others in Jesus' name.

Spotlight
MARY AND MARTHA

In Luke 10, Jesus and His disciples visited two sisters named Mary and Martha. Scripture says that "Martha welcomed him into her home" (v. 38).

The word *welcome* in this passage means to entertain hospitably.[1] However, Martha became sidetracked by the preparations and forgot about her guests while Mary sat at Jesus' feet, learning from Him. Martha became so focused on the details of hosting that she missed the reason why she had guests to begin with—so that they might learn from Jesus. This passage points to the heart of hospitality: to share the Bread of Life with others.

DAY 1: HOMESICK

Read John 14:1–7.

Worries. We've all got them. A negative by-product of being broken people living on a broken planet is that anxiety often bends our perception of the world around us, causing fears to well up and threaten to overwhelm us.

Jesus' disciples were made up of the same stuff you are. Though they walked and talked with Jesus, they still worried that their Savior would not come through.

John 14 describes one such worry-filled moment. Jesus was up-front with His disciples. He told them that He could not stay with them forever, at least not as the incarnate Son of God. Sensing His departure was coming soon, Peter asked an anxious question, "Lord, where are you going?" (John 13:36).

Rather than diagramming a theological case for the future or dismissing the disciples as naive or simple-minded, Jesus extended hospitality. *Home was on His heart.*

What worries you today? Make a list.

_____

_____

_____

_____

_____

In John 14:1, what wisdom did Jesus offer in response to Peter's worries?

_____

_____

It's worth paying attention to what Jesus *didn't* say.
- He didn't say that nothing bad would happen to Him or His disciples.
- He didn't say that He would alleviate all of life's pressures right away.
- He didn't say that the headlines would never be anxiety inducing.

What *did* Jesus say? Write down His words recorded in John 14:2–3.

_____

_____

_____

_____

_____

Why does this give us hope?

_____

_____

_____

_____

Weary traveler, Jesus is preparing a home for you.
Tired momma, Jesus is preparing a home for you.
Grieving widow, Jesus is preparing a home for you.
Sick sufferer, Jesus is preparing a home for you.
Worried woman, Jesus is preparing a home for you.

The hospitality Jesus showed to others as He walked the earth was just a foretaste of what He has for His followers in heaven. Without Him you had no hope of being welcomed in. Your sin separated you from the Father, but Jesus paid the penalty for your sin so that the doors of heaven could fling wide open for all who call upon His name. This is the ultimate example of true hospitality. Though you didn't earn it . . . Though you don't deserve it . . . Though you can never repay Him . . . Jesus has opened His heart and home to you.

Imagine the moment when you are finally welcomed into your heavenly home. What do you think it will be like?

_____
_____
_____
_____

Have you ever considered Jesus' words in John 14 an act of hospitality? Explain your answer.

_____
_____
_____
_____

Revist John 14:1–4 below. This time circle every instance of the word "prepare."

> "Don't let your heart be troubled. Believe in God; believe also in me. ² In my Father's house are many rooms. If it were not so, would I have told you that I am going to prepare a place for you? ³ If I go away and prepare a place for you, I will come again and take you to myself, so that where I am you may be also. ⁴ You know the way to where I am going."

Jesus doesn't need 2,000+ years to prepare a place for His people. With this in mind, why do you think He stated that He was preparing a place for the disciples?

_____
_____
_____

One of the things Jesus was emphasizing was His intentionality. He knew He was going to the cross. He stayed focused on His mission, knowing that someday all who surrendered their lives to Him would share His heavenly home permanently.

The God of the universe is eager to welcome you into the home He has prepared. *You are His invited guest.* Now *that's* hospitality!

Use the welcome mat below to write out the verse from John 14:1–4 that gives you the most hope today.

DAY 2: NO HEART HAS IMAGINED

Read 1 Corinthians 2:6–16.

Expectation—and occasionally nervous jitters—are part of the thrill of being welcomed into someone's home:
- What will they make for dinner?
- Will there be dessert?
- Will you play a board game or sit and visit?
- Who else will be there?

If you think waiting to step beyond the welcome mat of a friend or family member's home is exciting, imagine how your heart could be filled by meditating on the hospitality of heaven. Take a moment and describe what you think your heavenly home will be like. Write down any words or phrases that come to mind.

_____

_____

_____

_____

_____

While worldly "wisdom" is focused on what can be felt or experienced here and now, "God's hidden wisdom" compels us to look up and put our hope in something other than our temporary lives.

To help his readers think through this eternal grid, Paul gave a description of our heavenly home. Write down Paul's words found in 1 Corinthians 2:9.

_____

_____

In God's wisdom, He has chosen not to reveal all of the details about heaven. Though Scripture describes some things about our eternal home, much of it remains a mystery. Paul pointed out that if we closed our eyes and pictured the most beautiful place we've ever seen, if we reminisced about the most transcendent sound we've ever heard, if we spent days and weeks trying to imagine what heaven will be like . . . we'd barely scratch the surface. Whatever you think Jesus has in store for you in heaven, what He is preparing is infinitely more.

Why do you think God is preparing such a lavish home for His people?

_____
_____
_____
_____

Read Isaiah 64:1–5 from the ESV below. Underline the verse that sounds like Paul's words from 1 Corinthians 2:9.

> Oh that you would rend the heavens and come down,
>   that the mountains might quake at your presence—
> ² as when fire kindles brushwood
>   and the fire causes water to boil—
> to make your name known to your adversaries,
>   and that the nations might tremble at your presence!
> ³ When you did awesome things that we did not look for,
>   you came down, the mountains quaked at your presence.
> ⁴ From of old no one has heard
>   or perceived by the ear,
> no eye has seen a God besides you,
>   who acts for those who wait for him.
> ⁵ You meet him who joyfully works righteousness,
>   those who remember you in your ways.

Both Isaiah, a gifted Old Testament prophet who called God's people to pure worship of the one true God, and Paul, a New Testament missionary who called God's people to fully surrender their lives to Jesus, reminded their audiences of the awesomeness of God's character and unimaginable reality of heaven. Why do God's people need frequent reminders that heaven is more than we could ever envision?

_____
_____
_____
_____
_____

While your finite mind cannot fathom all that God has in store for you, you can know one important detail with absolute certainty—Jesus will be there to welcome you. How does this future reality shift how you see and respond to your current reality? Be specific.

_____
_____
_____
_____
_____

Jesus, thank You that You are preparing a place for me. Help me to live with anticipation for my heavenly home. I cannot wait to spend eternity in Your presence. Amen.

DAY 3: LET'S EAT!

Read Revelation 19.

It's a warm lasagna delivered to new parents.
It's a pot of chicken noodle soup taken to a sick neighbor.
It's a popcorn party in your dorm room.
It's a text to a hurting friend that says, "Let's meet for coffee."

Biblical hospitality doesn't always require opening the doors of your home nor does it demand photo-worthy meals. True hospitality is more of an attitude than a checklist. It requires reaching toward people in love—and if it happens to involve warm chocolate chip cookies, that's even better.

Revelation 19 describes an elaborate feast held in heaven. Look at the passage again and answer the questions below.

Will this be a large or small gathering? (v. 1)

_____

What will the mood be like? (v. 7)

_____

Will those in attendance dress up for the occasion? (v. 8)

_____

Will there be food? (v. 9)

_____

Jesus, our Bridegroom is preparing a feast for the Church, His Bride. Like many of the wedding receptions you may have attended, we will dress up in fine clothes, robes of righteousness purchased for us by our Savior (v. 8). We will celebrate our union with great joy (v. 7). Since God's Word describes this blessed event as "the marriage feast of the Lamb" (v. 9), we can also discern that we will feast!

Write out the passages below.

Deuteronomy 11:15

_____

_____

Song of Solomon 2:4

_____

_____

Psalm 22:26

_____

_____

Matthew 6:26

_____

_____

What theme do these passages share?

_____

_____

_____

One of the ways Jesus cares for us is by feeding us, and one thing we can anticipate about His heavenly hospitality is an elaborate feast to celebrate our forever union with Him.

Can you think of a time when being welcomed to a meal at someone's table ministered to you? Write about it.

_____
_____
_____
_____

How about a time when someone used food as a means to love and serve you well? Write about it.

_____
_____
_____
_____

Read Psalm 34:8 below. Circle which of your senses the psalmist points to.

> Taste and see that the LORD is good.
> How happy is the person who takes refuge in him!

Why do you think the psalmist used taste instead of highlighting our other senses?

_____
_____
_____
_____

Sure, you can cultivate hospitality by inviting people into a beautiful space or pulling them into a long hug and whispering "You matter" into their ear, but don't neglect their taste buds. Serving people with food mirrors the practical hospitality God has shown you.

What if delivering a pan of cinnamon rolls or inviting a new friend for a picnic could help them taste and see that the Lord is good and that He desires to fully satisfy them? What if simplicity made way for the sacred by sharing a meal that left someone hungry for more of Jesus? Love people; feed them good food. What if hospitality really is that uncomplicated?

Who do you know who needs encouragement this week?

_____
_____

What's one simple way you can use food as a means to extend the heart of hospitality toward them?

_____
_____
_____
_____

What's holding you back?

_____
_____
_____
_____

DAY 4: SHALOM AT HOME

Read Genesis 2:7–15.

Your welcome into your heavenly home may be days or decades away, but that doesn't mean it can't invade your life on earth. Focusing on God's hospitality keeps us motivated to use our homes to serve others well in Jesus' name.

Reflect on the Genesis 2 passage you just read. List several words that come to mind to describe the home God built for Adam and Eve.

_____

_____

_____

_____

Bible scholars often use the word *shalom* to define the garden God made for His first image bearers. It's a Hebrew word that means peace or wholeness.[2] God's intent was to welcome mankind into a place of unimaginable beauty, provision, and freedom. How does this sound similar to what you learned about heaven in this week's study?

_____

_____

_____

One way to build confidence in what God *will* do is remembering what He *has* done.

- He *has* created a home free of sin and shame.
- He *has* filled it with good food to eat and good work to do.
- He *has* made it possible for us to live in unbroken fellowship with Him and with each other.

Though sin has marred God's creation, we live in expectation of the restoration of shalom.

Read Revelation 22:1–4.

What is the same about this home and the one described in Genesis 2?

_____

_____

What is different?

_____

_____

What remarkable reversal is specifically promised in Revelation 22:3?

_____

_____

The end of the curse will mean the return of shalom. Peace will finally and forever be restored to our hearts and homes. What do you think that will be like?

_____

_____

_____

How did Jesus teach us to pray in Matthew 6:10? Rewrite His instructions in your own words.

_____

_____

_____

Prayer is just one way our heavenly hope infuses our lives on earth. Since we know that heaven is a place where we will be welcomed with love, we welcome others with love. Since we know it will be a place of peace, we strive to cultivate peaceful homes. As we long for the final return of shalom, we actively seek to extend shalom today.

The Valley of Vision, a classic collection of Puritan prayers, includes this plea:

> Sanctify and prosper my domestic devotion,
> instruction, discipline, example,
> that my house may be a nursery for heaven,
> my church the garden of the Lord,
> enriched with trees of righteousness of thy planting,
> for thy glory.[3]

Like a greenhouse protects seedlings as they grow, our homes can provide warmth and strength to others, making way for their hope in Christ to mature. Though we will continue to live in a broken world, our homes and resources can become outposts of shalom when we seek to use them to express the heart of hospitality to others.

Wrap up today's study by writing out the Puritan prayer above on a notecard and placing it somewhere in your home.

DAY 5: THE LEAST OF THESE

Read Matthew 25:31–46.

The people who walked and talked with Jesus seemed to have as much trouble envisioning the heaven He described as we do. Aware of the confusion in their hearts, He often used word pictures to explain what's to come.

In Matthew 25 Jesus described His return and eventual reign. At the end of the chapter He told about the coming judgment of people from every nation. He separated them into sheep, those who are welcomed into heaven, and goats, those who are sent away to eternal punishment. These are not literal sheep and goats but two types of people.

According to Matthew 25:35–40, what evidence of righteousness did Jesus call out in the sheep?

_____

_____

Does this sound like heavenly hospitality to you? Explain your answer.

_____

_____

_____

Review Matthew 25:41–46. What evidence of unrighteousness did Jesus call out in the goats?

_____

_____

_____

Was this group hospitable toward others? Explain your answer.

_____

_____

A clear view of the gospel is needed to understand this passage. Jesus wasn't saying that you can earn your way to heaven by doing good deeds for other people. Salvation comes by grace alone through faith alone in Christ alone. You cannot earn it even if you welcome every stranger and fix meals for others seven days a week. However, sacrificial giving is one way to celebrate the love and care you've already received from Jesus. In contrast, when you are stingy with your time and resources and don't love others well, it can be an indicator that you've missed the extravagant grace Jesus has lavished on you.

What kinds of people did Jesus mention as the recipients of care in these verses? Make a list.

_____

_____

_____

Do you see any similarities to the "who" of hospitality you learned about in Week 1?

_____

_____

True hospitality seeks to meet the needs of others as a way to put the love of God on display. While it's fine to open your home to a group of friends you love spending time with, biblical hospitality goes beyond that by actively pursuing those in need and welcoming them in.

The "least of these" could be:
- A single mom who is new to the area.
- The family with so many dietary restrictions they rarely get invited to dinner.

- Your pastor's wife who feels lonely in her role.
- A coworker who has trouble making friends.

The "least of these" could also be your husband with whom you're struggling to connect, your moody teenager who seems to be annoyed by everything you cook, or your toddler who manages to get more food on the floor than into her tummy.

Those who are the hardest to love may be those who most need to experience His love. This is one more way we can fold the shalom of heavenly hospitality into our lives on earth.

Read Romans 5:6–8. According to these verses, when did Jesus move toward us with radical love?

_____

_____

_____

He didn't insist we act loveable before He would love us. While we were busy running from Him in rebellion, He put love into action. He doesn't call us to love the "least of these" to earn His affections but as a means to show others how His love has transformed us.

Lord, thank You for loving me when I am weak. Thank You for dying for me before I could even ask for forgiveness. Help the gospel change the way I see and respond to the "least of these" around me. Amen.

Before closing your study today, consider who is hard for you to love. Ask the Lord to help you see them as the "least of these" and move toward them with godly affection.

"If I go away and prepare a place for you,
I will come again and take you to myself,
so that where I am you may be also."

—JOHN 14:3

Week 6
Your Most Honored Guest

Big Idea: Hospitality is using the resources God has given you to demonstrate His love to others.

INTRODUCTION

Lonely.
Fearful.
Suspicious.
Detached.

These words describe how many of us are operating in our current culture. Pain from past relationships motivates us to keep our distance. Headlines make us keep our guard up. In a world plagued by brokenness, rejection, and sin, there is a temptation to hunker down inside our own fortresses, barricaded behind high walls and locked doors.

These patterns have found their way into our churches and Christian communities. We see the same people week after week, nod, smile, exchange a few words . . . but do we really know each other? Do we share our struggles, needs, joys, and triumphs?

The heart of hospitality tears down our walls. When we look to Jesus we see that it's so much more than a mindset; it's a ministry. Hospitality breaks down barriers among believers *and* it's a weapon for reaching our wounded culture with the gospel.

Spotlight
RAHAB

Before the Israelites prepared to take possession of the land God had given them, Joshua sent two spies to Jericho to scope things out (Josh. 2). While there, the men chose to stay at the house of a prostitute named Rahab. When the authorities came looking for the Hebrew spies, Rahab helped them hide and eventually escape.

Later, when the city of Jericho fell, Rahab and her family did not perish along with everyone else. Hebrews 11:31 says that she was saved "by faith." Her willingness to express hospitality to the spies was *evidence* of her faith.

DAY 1: 10 REASONS WHY

Read Romans 12:9–13.

You could practice hospitality to impress your neighbors, hone your hostess skills, or spend time with others without breaking out of your comfort zone, but none of those reasons get to the heart of hospitality.

Based on what you've learned from this study, would you label Paul's words in Romans 12:13 as a command or suggestion? Explain your answer.

_____

_____

_____

Hospitality is close to the heart of God because it is a means for us to serve the saints, live out the gospel, and put His love on display. Here are ten more reasons why hospitality matters. Under each reason, write out the big idea of each passage that's listed.

1. Hospitality is a practical way to express the love of Christ.

    John 13:34–35

    Ephesians 3:17–19

2. Hospitality reflects the hospitable heart of God.

   Psalm 145:15–16

   Luke 12:24

3. Hospitality builds unity and community with other believers.

   Romans 12:13

   Galatians 5:13

4. The Bible promises rewards for those who practice hospitality.

   Hebrews 6:10

   Acts 20:35

5. God has commissioned you to reach toward the lost.

   Matthew 28:16–20

   Romans 10:12–15

6. Hospitality provides opportunities to walk closely with others.

   Ecclesiastes 4:9–12

   Galatians 6:2

7. Hospitality will confront your selfishness.

   Philippians 2:3

   1 Corinthians 10:24

8. Hospitality will help you resist materialism and focus on what lasts.

   Matthew 6:19–20

   2 Corinthians 9:6–8

9. Hospitality can help your children and grandchildren cultivate a love for ministry and a passion for serving other people.

   Matthew 5:16

1 Corinthians 11:1

10. God commands you to be hospitable.

   1 Peter 4:9

   Hebrews 13:2

Based on what you've learned from this study, can you add any additional reasons to show hospitality to the list?

_____
_____
_____
_____
_____
_____
_____

DAY 2: MAKING ROOM

Read Ephesians 2:14–18.

"There's room for you here." What a rare and beautiful thought.

Though heaven is only for the holy, Jesus made room for sinners through His sacrifice. Though Israelites are God's chosen people, His sacrifice made a way for people from every language, tribe, and nation to be saved (Rev. 7:9). He made room for you; you can make room for others.

In *The Spirit of Loveliness*, Emilie Barnes wrote,

> Hospitality is so much more than entertaining; so much more than menus and decorating and putting on a show. To me, it means organizing my life in such a way that there's always room for one more; an extra place at the table or an extra pillow and blanket; always a welcome for those who need a listening ear. It means setting aside time for planned fellowship and setting aside lesser priorities for impromptu gatherings.[1]

Can you think of other ways God has "made room" for you? List them.

_____

_____

_____

_____

We don't show hospitality to earn God's love but because we've already experienced it. His graciousness toward us motivates us to make room for others. Ultimately, the heart of hospitality takes us back to the cross where Jesus opened wide His arms and with His actions declared, "I will die in your place so that I can be your host. Welcome to my Father's house. There's room for you."

Reflect on Colossians 1:19–20. How does it shift your perception of hospitality to see it through the lens of the gospel?

_____
_____
_____
_____
_____

Reflect on these words from the Christmas carol, "Thou Didst Leave Thy Throne."

When the heav'ns shall ring and the angels sing,
At Thy coming to victory,
Let Thy voice call me home, saying "Yet there is room—
There is room at My side for thee."

My heart shall rejoice, Lord Jesus—
When Thou comest and callest for me.[2]

Take a moment to thank Him for making room for you through His sacrifice. Then ask Him to help you follow His example.

Father, as I look into the eyes of Jesus on the cross, I see His love for me. I am drawn to You because of what He has done for me. I pray that as others look into my eyes, as I open my heart and home to make room, that they would see the love of Jesus and understand the sacrifice He made on their behalf. I pray that they will find their home in Him. In Jesus name, amen.

DAY 3: BEACHSIDE BREAKFAST

Read John 21:1–14.

They were sad, confused, and scared—bone weary from the events of the past few days. They were with Him when He was arrested. They didn't worry then because He promised to set up a kingdom of His own. They heard rumors after He endured trial after trial. Their confidence began to buckle. Then, the unthinkable happened. Their Savior was beaten and mocked. They killed Him on a cross—a criminal's death.

What had happened? How did they lose their Savior?

Numb, they went back to what they knew.

"I'm going fishing," Peter told his grief-stricken friends.

"We're coming with you," they replied.

As you read the account in John 21, what strikes you?

_____

_____

_____

_____

What questions do you have?

_____

_____

_____

_____

Jesus could have surfed to His friends on a tidal wave of His own making. Instead, He welcomed them to the shore for a home-cooked breakfast. Again, we see that Jesus was, and is, the Ultimate Host.

Jesus welcomed lepers, adulteresses, and tax collectors. The worse the sinner, it seems, the wider His arms opened to receive them.

Read Luke 15:1–2.

How did the Pharisees respond to Jesus' hospitality toward others?

___

___

Based on your own experiences, why do you think they were so bothered?

___

___

To welcome others is Christlike, to exclude is Pharisaical. Jesus' ministry made it clear, He wanted to be with the people He came to save. Hospitality says, "I want your company. I want you to be with me. You may have been rejected by others. You may not receive me, but I receive you."

Can you think of other times in Jesus' earthly ministry when He received others in a hospitable way? Make a list.

___

___

These examples show what kind of relationship Jesus desires to have with you. He doesn't want it to be distant or strained. There is an infinite gap between a holy God and sinful man, but Jesus came to bridge that gap. He receives you with open arms.

Does Jesus' example convict you in any way? Write about it.

___

One practical way you can live out the heart of hospitality is by doing what Jesus did: make someone breakfast. It's a simple, heartfelt way to express that your arms are open. Make a plan below.

Who will you feed?

___

What will you cook?

___

When will you get together?

___

What do you hope they experience?

___

DAY 4: IT'S ALL HIS

Read Matthew 25:14–30.

Who owns your home? The answer isn't necessarily as simple as identifying whose name is on the deed. What's more:
- Who owns your time?
- Who owns your talents?
- Who owns your energy?

Our me-first culture would answer those questions with an adamant "I do!" You don't have to look far to find messages that insist that what's yours is yours and you should protect it at any costs.

The Bible calls us to a different mindset. In God's economy we are called to consider *stewardship* instead of ownership. Ownership declares, "This is mine, I've earned it," while stewardship says, "This is God's, He has graciously entrusted it to me." Ownership requires you to keep a tight grip on your possessions so they won't be taken from you, but stewardship opens your hands with the liberating truth that God gives and takes away.

Consider the parable you read in Matthew 25. What do you think Jesus was seeking to communicate about stewardship? Write down whatever comes to mind.

_____
_____
_____
_____
_____
_____
_____

Look up the passages listed below. Beside each reference write down the big idea Scripture is teaching.

Proverbs 24:1

___

Matthew 6:21

___

Luke 16:10–12

___

1 Timothy 6:7–8

___

James 1:17

___

1 Peter 4:10

___

How are biblical stewardship and biblical hospitality connected?

___
___
___
___

Consider the Matthew 25 parable once again. When it comes to the tools available to you to extend hospitality to others, what talents has God given you?

_____
_____

Are you investing those talents in ways that multiply God's kingdom? Explain your answer.

_____
_____

If not, what is hindering you?

_____
_____

Take away all of the trappings of unrealistic expectations, jam-packed schedules, and misdirected motivations, and hospitality is, at its core, an act of worship. It's recognizing that everything you have is a gift from God and being willing to share those gifts with others. It's sharing your dinner with neighbors because you know your food has been graciously provided by God. It's inviting a new mom over for coffee because you recognize your time as your greatest ministry asset. It's inviting a college student to join your family's Thanksgiving celebration because you remember what it's like to be away from your loved ones during the holidays.

Read Deuteronomy 10:14. According to this verse, who ultimately owns everything?

_____
_____
_____

How does this shift how you use your time, talents, and treasures?

_____

_____

_____

As you have worked through this study, have you experienced conviction in the area of hospitality? Write about it below.

_____

_____

_____

Have you experienced commendation, affirmation from God's Word that you are stewarding your gifts well? Write about it below.

_____

_____

_____

Though you've learned that biblical hospitality has little to do with seemingly effortless entertaining, perfect meals, or spotless houses, you've also learned that only Jesus demonstrated hospitality perfectly. As you follow His example, you will need His grace *and* you will need to trust Him with the fruit.

As you wrap up today's study, write out a prayer thanking God for the many blessings He's given you and expressing your desire to steward them well for His glory.

_____

_____

_____

DAY 5: THE BLESSING

Read Matthew 25:31–40.

Imagine hosting Jesus in your home. What would you feed the Bread of Life? How would you roll out the welcome mat for the High King of Heaven? How would you seek to honor the One who has given you everything?

You can't be among those who physically hosted Jesus while He walked the earth, but it is possible to honor Him through hospitality. The next time a guest comes to your door, keep in mind that Jesus is right there too. When you treat a guest well, you're serving your Savior.

Review Matthew 25:35–36. Was Jesus describing hospitality in these verses? Explain your answer.

_____
_____
_____

Look at the questions His teaching raised in verses 37–39. Why do you think they were confused?

_____
_____
_____

Record Jesus' answer from verse 40.

_____
_____
_____

Keep that passage in mind as we examine the blessings of hospitality. When we are hospitable, we don't just bless others but we receive blessings ourselves. Look up the passages below. Next to each reference write down the blessing the host received.

In Genesis 24, what blessings did Laban receive?

_____

_____

In Exodus 2, what blessings did the priest of Midian (Jethro) receive?

_____

_____

In 1 Kings 17, what blessings did the widow of Zarephath receive?

_____

_____

In Joshua 2, what blessings did Rahab receive?

_____

_____

What blessings have you experienced as you've shown hospitality to others? Add your thoughts to the list started below.

The blessings of being hospitable:
- Your children learn how to love and serve others.
- You say no to selfishness and grow in selflessness.
- You make new friends.
- Your bonds with friends and family are strengthened.
- You grow in gratitude toward others.

-
-
-
-
-
-
-

Despite the *many* blessings that come with true hospitality, the greatest gift is this: when you offer hospitality to God's people, you are offering hospitality to Jesus Himself.

Review Matthew 25:34–40 with that remarkable truth in mind. Circle the word "I" every time it appears in this passage.

> ³⁴ "Then the King will say to those on his right, 'Come, you who are blessed by my Father; inherit the kingdom prepared for you from the foundation of the world.
> ³⁵ "'For I was hungry and you gave me something to eat; I was thirsty and you gave me something to drink; I was a stranger and you took me in;
> ³⁶ I was naked and you clothed me; I was sick and you took care of me; I was in prison and you visited me.'
> ³⁷ "Then the righteous will answer him, 'Lord, when did we see you hungry and feed you, or thirsty and give you something to drink? ³⁸ When did we see you a stranger and take you in, or without clothes and clothe you?
> ³⁹ When did we see you sick, or in prison, and visit you?'
> ⁴⁰ "And the King will answer them, 'Truly I tell you, whatever you did for one of the least of these brothers and sisters of mine, you did for me.'"

To Jesus, your hospitality is personal. When you open your home to your Christian brothers and sisters, you're ultimately serving Him. One of the greatest rewards of hospitality is to know that in serving others, you have had the privilege of serving Jesus. That's remarkable on its own, but Scripture promises that God loves to bless His children.

Have you seen this to be true as you've extended hospitality?

_____

_____

As you close this study and begin to put into practice what God's Word teaches about hospitality, you can have confidence that it's not possible to outgive God. As you stretch out of your comfort zone to welcome a stranger, remember how God has welcomed you. As you add some chairs to the table to make room for others, give thanks that God has made room in heaven for you. And as you open your arms and heart wide to love others well, bask in the blessing of knowing that you've honored Jesus, your most honored Guest.

As we love others in Jesus' name, we do so in expectation of the day when our Savior welcomes us saying, "Come, you who are blessed by my Father; inherit the kingdom prepared for you from the foundation of the world" (Matt. 25:34).

For God was pleased to have
all his fullness dwell in him,
and through him to

reconcile

everything to himself,
whether things on earth
or things in heaven,
by making peace
through his blood,
shed on the cross.

—COLOSSIANS 1:19–20

Discussion Questions

WEEK 1: YOUR HOME IS A MISSION FIELD

1. Read Romans 12:9–21 aloud from several different translations. How would you sum up the main idea of this passage?
2. Have you ever considered your home as "set apart" for kingdom work? Explain.
3. Describe a time when you experienced genuine love. How did you know it was the real deal?
4. Who are the "one anothers" in your life? Make a list.
5. What kinds of people do you tend to extend hospitality to? How did this week's study stretch you in that area?

WEEK 2: EVIDENCE OF GENUINE LOVE

1. What is a practical way you can express the mercy you've received from Christ to others?
2. What keeps you from lovingly serving your family on a daily basis?
3. Do you tend to serve others with a happy heart? If not, what is your default heart posture?
4. What "as soon as" excuses do you tend to make about hospitality?
5. Revisit the chart on page 44. Discuss your responses with each other.

WEEK 3: GOD'S HEART FROM THE START

1. What is your typical response to unexpected visitors or interruptions? Why do you think you respond that way?
2. What does it mean to love your neighbor as yourself?
3. What are your hospitality hang-ups? Be specific.

4. Have you ever thought of God as the Ultimate Host? How has your thinking shifted this week?
5. How have you experienced the Lord's generosity in your life?

WEEK 4: THE BEAUTY OF HOSPITALITY

1. What is one of your favorite spaces in your home? Why do you love it?
2. Describe a time that you experienced the grace of God through the people of God.
3. Is it difficult for you to receive generous hospitality? Why do you think that is?
4. How does God use beauty to speak to you about His character?
5. How can you surround yourself and others with reminders of your heavenly home?

WEEK 5: YOUR HEAVENLY HOME

1. Take time to dream about what heaven will be like. What are you most looking forward to?
2. How does knowing Jesus is preparing a place for you encourage your heart today?
3. Why do you think we will feast in heaven? How does knowing that change your approach to food and hospitality on earth?
4. What are you doing to make your home "a nursery for heaven"? Share ideas.
5. What is the biggest area of heart change you've experienced through this study?

WEEK 6: YOUR MOST HONORED GUEST

1. Have your motivations for showing hospitality shifted? Tell the group how.
2. How has God made room for you? What difference has it made in your life?
3. What is the difference between *stewardship* and *ownership*? How does understanding this difference change your approach to hospitality?
4. What blessings have you experienced because you've shown hospitality to others?
5. What is one big idea you will take away from this study?

Notes

WEEK 1: YOUR HOME IS A MISSION FIELD

1. "Lexicon: Strong's G5382—*philoxenia*," Blue Letter Bible, accessed February 6, 2024, blueletterbible.org/lexicon/g5381/kjv/tr/0-1/.
2. Dorothy Kelley Patterson and Rhonda Harrington Kelley, *Women's Evangelical Commentary: New Testament* (Brentwood, TN: Holman Reference, 2011), 355.
3. William Arndt et al., *A Greek-English Lexicon of the New Testament and Other Early Christian Literature* (Chicago, IL: University of Chicago Press, 2000), 254.
4. Hayley Mullins and Erin Davis, *Living Out the One Anothers of Scripture* (Niles, MI: Revive Our Hearts, 2020).
5. "#103: Polycarp's Martyrdom," Translated by J.B. Lightfoot. Abridged and modernized by Stephen Tomkins. Edited and prepared for the web by Dan Graves. Christian History Institute, accessed February 6, 2024, christianhistoryinstitute.org/study/module/polycarp.
6. James Strong, *A Concise Dictionary of the Words in the Greek Testament and The Hebrew Bible* (Bellingham, WA: Logos Bible Software, 2009), 20.

WEEK 2: EVIDENCE OF GENUINE LOVE

1. Donald K. Campbell. "Galatians." In *The Bible Knowledge Commentary: An Exposition of the Scriptures*, edited by J. F. Walvoord and R. B. Zuck, vol. 2 (Wheaton, IL: Victor Books, 1985), 607.
2. Craig Blomberg, *Matthew (Volume 22) (The New American Commentary)* (Nashville: Broadman & Holman Publishers, 1992), 232.

WEEK 3: GOD'S HEART FROM THE START

1. John Owen, *Hebrews (The Crossway Classic Commentaries)* (Wheaton, IL: Crossway Books, 1998), 257.
2. John Piper, "Love Your Neighbor as Yourself, Part 2," Desiring God, May 7, 1995, www.desiringgod.org/messages/love-your-neighbor-as-yourself-part-2.
3. Andrew Murray, *The Believer's Absolute Surrender* (Minneapolis: Bethany, 1985), 78.
4. Dane Ortlund. "Psalm 23." In *ESV Devotional Psalter* (Wheaton, IL: Crossway Books, 2017).
5. Allen P. Ross. "Psalms." In *The Bible Knowledge Commentary: An Exposition of the Scriptures*, edited by J. F. Walvoord and R. B. Zuck, vol. 1 (Wheaton, IL: Victor Books, 1985), 812.

WEEK 4: THE BEAUTY OF HOSPITALITY

1. Darrell L. Bock, *Acts: Baker Exegetical Commentary on the New Testament* (Grand Rapids, MI: Baker Academic, 2007), 213.
2. Bock, *Acts*, 215.
3. Bock, *Acts*, 215.
4. Bock, *Acts*, 742.
5. Stanley D. Toussaint. "Acts." In *The Bible Knowledge Commentary: An Exposition of the Scriptures*, edited by J. F. Walvoord and R. B. Zuck, vol. 2 (Wheaton, IL: Victor Books, 1985), 429.
6. Adapted from Nancy DeMoss Wolgemuth, *Brokenness, Surrender, Holiness: A Revive Our Hearts Trilogy* (Chicago: Moody Publishers, 2008), 60–63.

WEEK 5: YOUR HEAVENLY HOME

1. "Lexicon: Strong's G5264—*hypodechomai*," Blue Letter Bible, accessed September 20, 2023, blueletterbible.org/lexicon/g5264/kjv/tr/0-1/.
2. Dr. Aviezer Ravitzky, "Shalom: Peace in Hebrew," My Jewish Learning, myjewishlearning.com/article/shalom/.
3. Arthur Bennett, *The Valley of Vision: A Collection of Puritan Prayers & Devotions* (Edinburgh: Banner of Truth Trust, 2002), 208–209.

WEEK 6: YOUR MOST HONORED GUEST

1. Emilie Barnes, *The Spirit of Loveliness* (Eugene, OR: Harvest House Publishers, 1992), 126–127.
2. E.S. Elliot, "Thou Didst Leave Thy Throne," 1864.

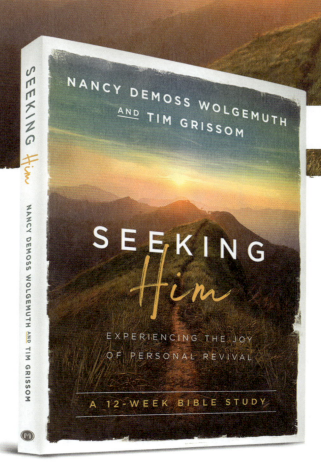

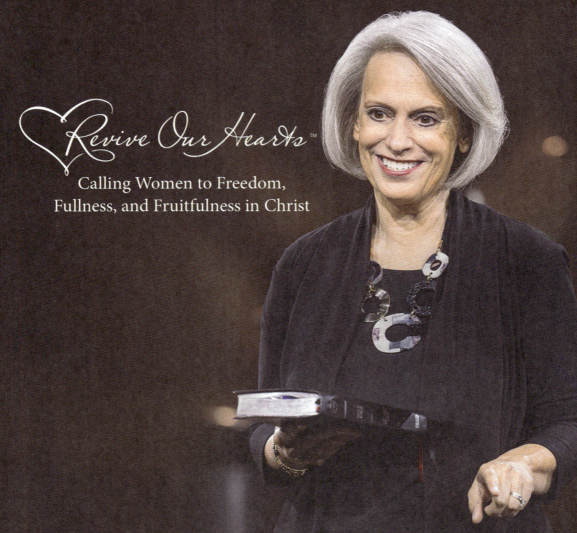

RAHAB

TRACING THE THREAD OF REDEMPTION

A six-week Bible study based on the teaching of Nancy DeMoss Wolgemuth